THE SPOTTER'S GUIDE
TO
THE MALE SPECIES

Library of Congress Cataloging in Publication Number:
2005934971

ISBN: 1-59474-129-8

Printed in China

Typeset in Baskerville & Century Gothic

Designed by Lindsey Johns

Conceived and produced by
Quid Publishing
Level Four
Sheridan House
114 Western Rd
Hove BN3 1DD
England
www.quidpublishing.com

Distributed in North America by Chronicle Books
85 Second Street
San Francisco, CA 94105

10 9 8 7 6 5 4 3 2 1

Quirk Books
215 Church Street
Philadelphia, PA 19106
www.quirkbooks.com

Picture credits: Fig 1.4 © Tim McGuire/Corbis,
Fig. 1.7 © Zave Smith/Corbis, Fig. 2.3 © Jon
Feingersh/Corbis, Fig. 7.6 © Karl Weatherly/Corbis

THE SPOTTER'S GUIDE
TO
THE MALE SPECIES

Juliette Wills

QUIRK
BOOKS

CONTENTS

Introduction 6

SECTION ONE
APPEARANCE AND PLUMAGE
Clothes 10

Hair 14

Shoes 18

Accessories 22

SECTION TWO
CHARACTER TRAITS
What He Says 26

Body Language 30

Who He's With 34

How He Gets Around 38

SECTION THREE
HIS NATURAL HABITAT
Living Room 42

His Bedroom 46

The Kitchen 50

The Bathroom 54

SECTION FOUR
HIS FEEDING HABITS
What He Eats 58

What He Drinks 62

When He Feeds 66

How He Obtains His Food 70

SECTION FIVE
HIS JOB

What He Does for a Living 74
What He Earns 78
His Ambitions/Aspirations 82
If He Is Unemployed 86

SECTION SIX
HIS MATING HABITS

Pick-Up Lines 90
His Physical Approach 94
Preening and Preparation 98
After Mating 102

SECTION SEVEN
BEHAVIOUR PATTERNS

With His Friends 106
With His Family 110
Migratory Habits 114
Nocturnal Activity 118

SECTION EIGHT
HIBERNATION INSTINCTS

What Films and Television He Watches 122
What Computer Games He Plays 126
What Music He Listens To 130
Where He Hibernates 134

Appendix One: Glossary of Terms 138
Appendix Two: Quick-Reference Guide 140
Index 142
About the Author 144

INTRODUCTION

How many times have you judged a man's worth by the car he drives or the job he has? Don't pretend you're not like that. We all are. The female species wasn't handed out an extra helping of the judgemental genes for nothing, you know. OK, so seeing a man whiz past in a brand new Porsche doesn't require too much brain power to work out that he might be better off than one who cycles past on an old rust bucket. It's intuition that you can't buy—and that's where this book comes in handy.

Meeting Mr. Right

You may be wondering what you're doing wrong when it comes to meeting suitable men. The answer is that what's suitable for one woman won't be for the next. Some women are only interested in what a man has in his wallet–and I don't mean pictures of Jessica Alba or a discount card for the local dry cleaner–whilst others care more about a man's morals and values.

That's not to say that you can't have both, but the male species is a complicated bundle of fat, sinew, muscle, and hair. On some males all the aforementioned are in the places they should be; on others, not so. Commonly misplaced items include hair in the nostrils and on the back rather than on the head. Ugh.

Judging the goods

So how can you tell at first glance whether a man will make you dizzy with excitement or dizzy with nausea? Will you be engulfed by lust or mistrust? Can you tell if he likes you just by looking at the way he's standing? Does how he treats his mother relate to how he'll treat you? Will you be asking yourself pertinent questions such as these the next time you spot someone you like the look of? After reading this book you will. What's more, it's small enough to slip surreptitiously into your handbag, so you can take it wherever you go and match the object of your interest to the description in the book. Be sure not to make a move until you've read it–unless you enjoy living on the edge by, say, dating a serial killer, or even just a total loser. In fact, they're pretty much the same thing, only the serial killer knows he's a loser and it made him really cross, which is why he started killing people.

Your indispensable guide

The Spotter's Guide to the Male Species covers every aspect of the male psyche, from his characteristics, appearance, and body language through to survival tactics, his habitat, and his job, or even lack of one. You'll soon be able to pin-point a man's good and bad points within seconds, saving you and your friends the embarrassment of dating a chump. You might look at a bad date as only wasting one evening, but it's an evening you could have been spending with your future husband rather than another woman's current husband. Ouch.

So now you have it. Your at-a-glance reference guide to every type of male out there, including those who really shouldn't be out there. From pulling you away from a man in novelty socks to screaming, "Danger! Do not approach!" to men in cowboy boots, *The Spotter's Guide* is your indispensable best friend. The information contained in these pages could save you from committing such travesties as dating men who don't wash their bed clothes, who eat food from under the sofa, and who think it's OK to wear sweaters tied over their shoulders.

You'll wonder how you ever managed without it.

APPEARANCE
AND PLUMAGE

CLOTHES

We all have bad days when we're running late and throw on whatever's lying on the bedroom floor, be it pyjamas or the dog's blanket. Some men, though, dress like this all the time. So what can you tell about a man from the way he is dressed? A lot. Trust me. If he's wearing . . .

Novelty socks or tie

(Fig. 1.1) You'll need a close look at this one. Not to decide whether to go for it or not, but just so that you can take in the full horror and keep the moment clear in your mind for the rest of your life. Whether it's Homer Simpson, Fred Flintstone, Mickey Mouse, or even Dennis the Menace, back away slowly, then run for the hills. Desperate to appeal to your humorous side, this particular male will fire off a succession of terrible jokes to tempt you into his path and then pull up his trouser leg or hold out his tie to make certain you know just how "crazy" he is. Probably works as a telemarketer and lives with his parents, mustering the courage to flee the nest but, like a week-old lion cub, unable to fend for himself (let alone you).

Fig. 1.1 Pray day and night that you never stumble across a pair like this.

Anything made of linen

He's ill. You'll know that because he'll have been in a hospital waiting room recently and picked up a dog-eared copy of *GQ* from 1987. Inside he'll have spotted a handsome male in a white linen shirt, probably advertising aftershave or diamond watches, with said male lounging on a leather sofa with tanned, pedicured, and air-brushed feet and a Labrador by his side. He'll have decided that linen is the way forward, not taking into account that the advertisement is extremely old and that he is totally unlike the model in the ad. An identity crisis is apparent. A breed apart, this one—make sure he stays that way.

Beige trousers and pale denim shirt

Ah, the classic "boarding school" look as favoured by Ivy League boys and managing directors who can't quite let go on "dress down Friday." Chinos say that this male plays safe, probably in and out of the bedroom, and sticks to what he knows—and what he knows is that you can't go wrong with brushed denim and beige. But you can, particularly if it's topped off with a yellow Ralph Lauren sweater worn over the shoulders. Is he on a yacht or returning from a tennis match? Even if he is, the sweater over the shoulders is unacceptable. The sparrow of the man world. Yawn.

Stone-washed jeans and fringed leather jacket

Wey-hey, what do we have here? George Michael circa 1986, Michael Flatley circa 2006, or an ordinary guy with a frazzled mind who somewhere along the line forgot to buy some new clothes? Stone-washed jeans are worse than blood-stained jeans in my book, and fortunately this is my book. The "crims" in Michael Jackson's "Beat It" video wore stone-washed denim. And bandannas. They were meant to scare us, and they did. Not because they looked tough, but because they looked ridiculous.

Fig. 1.2 An outfit you can't possibly go wrong with. Should be supplied in combination with at least one tattoo.

White T-shirt, Levi's

(Fig. 1.2) You can't go wrong with this. Honestly. A brooding James Dean in *Rebel Without a Cause* or Matt Dillon in *Rumblefish*. It's a look that has been around for years, and there's a reason for that. It's a classic, manly look, and if worn by someone of, say, Mexican descent who's eating a taco having just pulled into a diner in his '57 Chevy, then it's enough to give you heart murmurs. Swallow or heart-and-dagger tattoos complete the look; Celtic symbols, Chinese writing, or barbed-wire bands kill it. A pure hunk of old-fashioned male, you may have to cook his steak and answer to his every whim, but he'll be certain to make it all worth your while. . . .

White suit, black shirt, white tie

"Look how unconventional I am," says the male to the suit. And he's right. Although everyone else who has to look smart but doesn't want to wear navy blue or charcoal grey may be thinking the same thing. A handsome man with cash to spare can carry this look off, as long as his hair and shoes aren't competing for attention with the suit. It smacks of confidence, of course, but in a good way. If he hits a dog when he's driving, he won't stop to pick it up and carry it to the pavement. You may think him heartless; he will think, "I'm wearing a white suit!" Like a cute albino pigeon, he gets noticed for all the right reasons.

Hooded top, big jeans

(Fig. 1.3) If he's 40, he's got issues. He thinks he's still a teenager, even though when he was a teenager everyone was wearing orange flares and purple tank tops. If he's under 25, he can get away with it, depending on how baggy the top and the jeans are. He may have poor circulation, and is therefore wearing all his clothes at once, or else he's down with the skate crowd, and if he didn't wear jeans 18 sizes too big and worn lower than his underwear he'd have no social life. As it is, his social life is probably no different than when he was eight: go to the park, scare old ladies, eat a bag of chips, slouch a lot, and ride about on a skateboard. Avoid as you would a swarm of locusts.

Fig. 1.3 A hooded top and ill-fitting baggy jeans– he's 35 but still can't dress himself properly. Buy him a belt for Christmas.

A gorilla suit

He might be between jobs. Perhaps he was once a high-powered executive and fell on hard times, and this blip in his career is a chance for him to try out "new directions," such as handing out leaflets for the local zoo or standing outside a fried-chicken shop dressed, the next day, as a chicken. Any man game enough to dress as a member of the animal kingdom deserves a moment of your time. If he actually looks like a primate once the suit comes off, forget it. Bear in mind he may also be a stripper. It's up to you to decide whether that's a good thing or not. If you're in the rainforest, however, it may well just be a gorilla. Best to ask.

HAIR

If the eyes are the window to the soul, then the hair is the curtains around it. Delilah cut off Samson's and ruined his life, but that was in the Bible, not this book. So how can you tell a man by his hair? Easy! If he has . . .

A crew cut

(Fig. 1.4) Ah, a man who believes that hair products are for sissies and that combs take up valuable space in the pocket where a penknife could be. Either he's in the armed forces, used to be in the armed forces, or thinks he's in the armed forces. The giveaway here is that if there's a war going on, he'll be behind a sandbag or inside a tank, not propping up the bar in the dive around the corner. Other possibilities are that he's growing out his hair after a bad case of lice, an incident involving gum, or he's so manly that he believes doing anything other than running a hand over the top of his head to check if it's still there is for girls. He could be right. A tough, no-nonsense male who leads where others follow.

Dreadlocks

(Fig. 1.5) We've got two distinct types here. First is the Afro-Caribbean dreadlock, normally worn for religious reasons. It happens to also look very cool, especially under a brightly coloured woolly hat. It says he's laid back and proud of his roots, hair and otherwise, and is confident and content with his lot. Then there are the rope-like dreadlocks with bits of old string and ribbon (and possibly mice) running through it. He doesn't wash very much and may pick at his matted hair like a primate searching for ticks–and will probably find some. He'll also protest about roads being built, live in a tree, and tell you off for using lipstick because it's made from whale blubber.

Fig. 1.4

Fig. 1.5

Fig. 1.6

Fig. 1.7

Spiky hair

(Fig. 1.6) Short. Not tall. Of below average height. Vertically challenged. Yes, this male has growing problems, and the problem is that he hasn't grown. He may well be wearing Cuban heels at the other end. Desperate to gain an inch or two, he'll spend all his cash on gel, spray, and fixing products, and be sure to stand clear of open fires. Small flies will get stuck between the hairs and lose the will to live as they struggle to free themselves from the gloop. May also take your eye out if you lean in to whisper sweet nothings. His friends will have the same style, and will hunt in spiky packs, like coiffed wolves.

Long hair

(Fig. 1.7) Ugh. And I'll say that again: ugh. If it's black with red streaks in it, he wishes he were Marilyn Manson. If it's blonde and wavy, he wishes he were Marilyn Monroe. Either way, you'd better be careful. Long, straight, shiny hair is almost worse than long, straggly, dirty hair. The first screams, "I yearn to be as beautiful as my mother/girlfriend/transsexual father," and one day, he probably will. The second says, "I'm rebelling and I like rock music," or "I'm part of a scientific experiment to see what happens if you don't wash your hair," and for that, see "Dreadlocks" (at left). An inexcusable lack of preening.

15

Highlights

(Fig. 1.8) Oh dear, there really is no excuse for this. Having your hair highlighted is a conscious decision. You have to book the appointment, and then spend hours in a chair with bits of foil on your head whilst flicking through puzzle magazines. What kind of man does this? The kind who thinks he's going to attract you by having strands of his hair painted gold. Worse still, it could be green, either from trying to do it himself or going swimming. And if he's got highlights and goes swimming, he's really got too much time on his hands. And no wonder–he's unlikely to have a girlfriend. Like a bird who spends all day collecting twigs and putting them in a tree only for the tree to get cut down– this hair "style" is a total waste of time and effort.

A quiff

(Fig. 1.9) My personal favourite. The reason why Elvis Presley still sells records today? OK, the music's great, but the hair–that's in a league of its own too. It may leave grease marks all over your pillows, and some pomade even turns your fingers brown, but there's no better sight than a thick, black, greased-up pompadour to lift the spirits. Not to be confused with short man's spiky-haired syndrome, this is an old-fashioned, no-nonsense affair. A proud male, he takes his time to get it right, but will always leave a trail in his wake. This male will be able to mend cars, carry you home when your feet hurt, and with one swift swipe of his comb, send your heart racing. Not for the faint-hearted.

Bowl cut

(Fig. 1.10) "Mommy, my bangs are in my eyes and I can't see to complete my jigsaw puzzle," cries the wearer of this style. Either he's trying to save money by cutting it himself around a cereal bowl just like Mom used to, or he's going for the 1960s beatnik look in the hope of attracting a woman who looks like Jane Birkin or Brigitte Bardot. He lives in a dream world where he thinks sensible hair shows that he

Fig. 1.8

Fig. 1.9

Fig. 1.10

Fig. 1.11

can be trusted, isn't superficial, and will be interested in *you*, rather than *him*. In reality, it just means he looks hideous. Likely to be separate from the main pack

None

(Fig. 1.11) Has it all fallen out, or is it so closely shaved that it feels like sandpaper? You'll only know if you touch, and that's not recommended. A shiny head may be oily or hot to the touch if under lights. A balding man sensible enough to shave what's left of his hair is a man worth getting to know—he's realised his limits and will try harder to woo you than a man with a lot of hair. If he's ugly, he may look like a thug; if he's pretty, he may look like a girl with no hair. It's a close call. Whatever the case, he won't be pinching your shampoo and conditioner, and that can only be a bonus. Just check with the local police to make sure no prisoners have recently escaped. If he's wearing a bright-orange pyjama-like outfit with "Property of Corrections Department" stamped on the lapel, run like the wind.

SHOES

They, whoever "they" may be, say you can't judge a book by the cover but you can judge a man by his shoes. And they're right. Nothing gives away a man's secrets more than his footwear. Before you even consider making eye contact with a man, you must lower your gaze to ground level to see what's what. If he's wearing . . .

Expensive sneakers
(Fig. 1.12) He's obviously style-conscious and may have some money in the bank, or else he's broke but desperate to keep up with the latest trends. Could go either way, this one, so check other accessories, such as the watch or cell phone, for the answer. If the sneakers are gleaming white, then he's bound to be precious about them. This suggests a lack of impulsive behaviour–in other words, he's not going to take up your offer of a walk on the beach or a fumble in the woods with these babies on his feet. Probably works in TV/design/music, where if he wore the "wrong" sneakers he'd be shunned by the pack.

Fig. 1.12

Fig. 1.13

Fig. 1.14

Fig. 1.15

Right: Let the feet (or rather the footwear) do the talking.

Beaten-up Converse

(Fig. 1.13) Aah, a casual air suggests an easy-going temperament, and classic footwear hints at a man who's happy with himself—he has no need to impress and clearly chooses comfort over anything else. An air of "I'm ready for a quick game of basketball if you are" adventure is most alluring, unless, of course, his shoes are covered in chewing gum and are so beaten up they're a health hazard. There's a fine line between "relaxed" and "diseased." Probably works in a record shop/doesn't work at all.

Shoes or boots with a square toe

(Fig. 1.14) Hmm, a funny one, this. Either he's trying to be "different" and stand out from the crowd, or he's desperate to show he's no mama's boy and is rebelling from his Sunday school days, when he was forced to wear sensible black lace-up shoes with a round toe. Whose feet are square at the end? One must wonder whether he believes the theory that men with big feet have more than just big socks and is trying to make himself more attractive to ladies for that reason. Not suitable for the large footed male anyway—nobody wants to date Krusty the Clown. Probably a real estate agent or works in a men's shoe shop that had square-toed ones on special offer. Thinks he's it, but he isn't.

Snakeskin or white leather shoes

(Fig. 1.15) "Notice me!" scream his feet, forced into unsuitable attire like a small child strapped reluctantly into its stroller. He's either gay, brave, stupid, or all three, but until you get a closer look at the rest of him, it's hard to say which. He's the kind of man who walks into a club, stops just before he gets to the bottom of the stairs, and pauses to see if people look at him. With those kind of shoes they will, but for all the wrong reasons. He may think he's "crazy" and "out there"; you may think he's just daft. Peacocks look great when they show off—that's because they don't wear white leather shoes. Idiots do.

Black loafers

(Fig. 1.16) Sensible, smart, and, if they're Italian (I know you can't tell from a distance, but try), this man's a proper gentleman. His mother probably taught him how to do his own washing and ironing, and he might even be able to pour his own milk on his cereal in the mornings. The black loafer suggests an air of innocence and responsibility, plus it usually means he's got to match his socks up for the horrible moment when he sits down and hitches up his trousers at the knee, exposing the ankle–clumsy, thin, and pink like a flamingo's. It's not a look I favour, but Elvis wore loafers, so it can't be all bad. Saying that, though, Elvis could have worn a red jumpsuit and still looked great. Oh, he did.

Cowboy boots

(Fig. 1.17) There's really no excuse unless he is actually a cowboy, and if you're not in Texas or Nevada, then it's unlikely that he is. Brad Pitt in *Thelma & Louise* wasn't a cowboy as such, but he managed to carry it off, and he's the only man in history aside from Clint Eastwood who can.

Fig. 1.16

Fig. 1.17

Fig. 1.18

Above: The good, the bad, and the ugly of the footwear world. The loafer-wearer may be approached with safety; the others should be avoided at all costs.

Avoid this man at all costs—he's either headlong into stage two of a midlife crisis (stage one being the sports car) or he's in a band that hasn't made it. Unless, of course, he's Jon Bon Jovi, but even then he's had his day and should know better. Worn with jeans, by the way, is bad enough, but if they're worn with trousers, then he needs medical attention, fast. This kind of creature should be extinct by now.

Sandals or flip-flops

(Fig. 1.18) How's a man going to defend himself, never mind look out for you, if he's not wearing protective footwear? Toes on show? Vulnerability at its worst. You can't run, and you certainly can't hide. What's more, there are probably, ooh, seven men in the entire world who have pleasant toes, and that's at a push. First, they're hairy. Second, the toenails are usually bruised from playing football or kicking walls/doors in frustration when their team loses at football. Third, well, need I go on? A Birkenstock sandal in brown or white is excusable if worn on a very hot day or on holiday by a man with a natural golden tan; cheap, plastic, barely there flip-flops are a no-no whatever the circumstances, even if it does leave him open to picking up fungal infections at the swimming pool.

Nothing

This depends on whether he's indoors or not. Inside, it's still risky given men's hideous feet, but better than seeing them clad in a pair of slippers. If he's outside, then he's either homeless—and you can probably tell that if his feet are rotting and black and on the end of legs that are wrapped in newspaper—or else he may be the victim of shoe crime. He'll have to be warm-blooded, whatever the issue. Remember Carrie in *Sex and the City* being held up in a Manhattan side street for her designer stilettos? It's unlikely he'd have been wearing Jimmy Choo ankle-strap sandals, but you never know. Tramp or tranny? You wouldn't really want to go out with either.

ACCESSORIES

I once knew a jewellery designer who wore no jewellery. Despite him being able to advertise his business upon his fingers, ears, around his wrists and his neck, he chose not to. Sensible guy. The humble robin simply wows us with his red breast. He has no need for a medallion. So what do his accessories really say about him?

Cell phone

Does it take pictures? Does is make a noise to wake him up in the morning and send him a message to remind him to go to work once he's woken up? Does it store ex-girlfriend's names under men's names like "Bob" or "Dave," even though he doesn't know anyone called Bob or Dave? Is it in his pocket, or on the table? If it's on the table, he's showing off, and it probably has a satellite navigation system and a chewing-gum dispenser in it. If it's in his pocket, he's going to be able to pay some attention to you rather than his phone. Put it this way—if you can't see one, that's a good thing. A creature happy left to his own devices, quite literally.

Fig. 1.19 If his phone can take photos, why can't his camera take calls? Over-elaborate gadgets like these are for fools.

Portable music player

Whether it's a simple Walkman which takes cassettes and hasn't been seen on anyone under 35 this decade or a state-of-the-art, small-as-a-stamp, computer-compatible miracle with earplugs bigger than its whole self, this says so much about men as a species. Gadgetry exists for the sole purpose of men being able to display, rather like a peacock, their ability to understand things made of metal with switches and buttons. A passion for music is a good thing, unless you hear him singing along to Michael Bolton. Cassettes show a love for all things retro, so if you're an older woman you might be in with a shout; technical wizardry implies a magpie-like penchant for all things shiny. Likely to make a loud hawking sound should you try to pick it up.

Watch

If he's wearing one, it's a good sign– it means he can tell the time. However, if you get up close and it's got Mickey Mouse pointing his over-sized fingers at the numbers, then that's debatable. A diving watch with 87 different dials and a compass attached is unnecessary unless he's actually a diving instructor. A digital watch is all very well, but implies he hasn't got the time in the first place to work out what time it is on his own; you could well find he doesn't have the time for you either. An antique watch means he's sentimental, as it's probably been inherited from his grandfather. A pocket watch, on the other hand, just means he's mental.

Wallet

For many women, this is the most important accessory known to man, and used by man. It is, to you, the king of accessories, as it tells you whether he's old enough to have a credit card, sensible enough not to have more than one credit card, whether said credit card is one of those cool black and silver ones (bingo!), or whether the only card in there at all is from the back of a cigarette packet and says "Remember to report back to prison by 5 p.m." If it's black or brown leather and stacked with $20 bills, you're in luck. He's able to look after you, nurture you, and provide you with expensive shoes. Well, either that or he's just robbed someone. Photos of non-celebrity women will probably be his girlfriend or wife. It's kind of a good giveaway, but it's worth straining your neck to check for when he flips it open to pay for your vodka and tonic.

Keys

Always a good sign that he's got somewhere to live, unless the keyring says "Sunrise Trailer Park," in which case, it doesn't count. If there's no apparent signs of keys, it's likely he doesn't need to take them when he goes out because his mother or his wife will be there to let him in. Keyrings that are useful, such as penknives, torches, or mini stun guns, suggest a man who's prepared for trouble–but whether he's prepared *for* it or prepared to *start* it won't be so obvious.

Jewellery

Jewellery is not good. A watch tells the time, a necklace tells you he has a neck. What's the point? On women, necklaces are traditionally worn to draw attention to the cleavage. I would hope that most men don't have cleavage, and that if they did, they certainly wouldn't want to draw attention to it. One ring is acceptable–a wedding ring is obviously a good sign that he's taken, as is a peculiar white band of skin on an otherwise tanned hand. Worst offenders? Those hideous bits of leather worn around the neck or wrist with a supposed shark's tooth attached. Shark's tooth from a grapple with a great white when surfing off Bondi? Nah, he bought that in the mall last weekend. And don't even get me started on mangy bits of thread worn around the wrist–"It's for religious reasons," he'll say. No, it's not.

CHARACTER
TRAITS

WHAT HE SAYS

"It ain't what you say, it's the way that you say it," apparently, but what he says plays a part in communication. "You're pretty" is always nice to hear, however it's said (unless it's said by an old tramp). "You're dumped" is never going to sound good, no matter how it's said. Here are some clues to how members of the male species give away secrets about themselves without even realising . . .

His first words

(Fig. 2.1) I don't mean "mommy" when he was two; I'm talking about the first thing he says to you when he calls. Picture the scenario. He dials your cell phone. You see his name come up, so you know who it is. You have control, even though he knows who he's calling, simply by deciding whether to answer or not. "Hello?" you say, slightly inquisitively, as if to give the impression that men ring you all day so how the hell do you know who it is unless he announces himself. He says, "Hi, it's me." Aaagh! Not so bad when you've been married for 10 years, but after one date? Dreadful behaviour. He thinks he's already done all the hard work and that he's got you exclusively until he decides otherwise. Presumptuous and obnoxious, unless he's got a name which is really hard to pronounce, like Xavier, and can't actually say it, in which case he's an idiot for not learning it or changing it.

Fig. 2.1 "Hello, it's me," when you're not even married? The nerve of it!

Fig. 2.2 "And while you're at it, love, shove some coins in the parking meter would you?" Not what you want to hear.

To those in the public service sector

(Fig. 2.2) You're in a restaurant, and while you push salad leaves around your plate for fear of consuming any calories, he decides that his steak is overcooked. How does he summon the attention of the waitress? Does he whistle at her through two fingers, cock his head, and make a "my steak is rubbish" face, or raise a finger–not the middle one–when she walks past to catch her eye and smile when she comes over? Anything other than the last action is appalling. He can stop smiling once she gets to him and explain politely that his sirloin is "a little well done for my liking, and I did order it medium," and that's fine. You've got yourself a true gentleman. If, however, he spits in her face, throws the plate and said steak upon the floor, and screams, "You'll never work in this town again!" to nobody in particular, then he's insane. A pretty easy one, that.

At the drive-thru

You pull up to the intercom thing at the drive-thru. He wants a strawberry milkshake, large fries, and a hamburger. Fair enough–don't we all? But how does he ask for it? If he says, "Hi," first of all, then he has the decency to recognise that there's a person at the other end, and it might mean he once worked somewhere similar and realises the importance of good manners. If he says "please" and "thank you," you've got yourself a lovely young, or even old, man. Marry him immediately. If he barks his order at the machine, says, "What? I can't hear a word you're saying, you complete idiot," then quickly step out of the car, because you've got an American Psycho on your hands. If he does the nice things and lets you sip his milkshake, congratulate yourself on an excellent choice. Unless, of course, this is actually your first date. That's not so hot.

When he meets your best friend

A tricky one, this. If he says too many nice things about her, he'll be accused of having the hots for her. If he doesn't say anything nice about her, he'll be accused of hating her. If he only says something mean about her, he may end up with a punch in the face. A clever lady, though, might deduce from an insult that he is, in fact, working backwards to attempt to cover up the fact that he is in love with her. Oh dear. Refresh yourself with the "Body Language" section (page 30) for this one. Tugging his earlobe, stepping from one foot to the other, and saying, "I thought Susan was truly ugly; I'd sooner kiss a cat," may be too much of a protestation. A simple "Yeah, she was nice" is what a sensible man should say, and he probably means it. Just don't ask him if she's prettier than you. He might get it wrong and say yes.

When you ask him if he ever wants to get married

(Fig. 2.3) If he answers with, "No, I'd rather gouge out my kidneys with a rusty spoon," then you've got a pretty good idea he's not going to be whisking you off to the wedding chapel just yet. Or probably ever. If he makes a face like he's just eaten a weevil, then he may one day be swayed into thinking it's for him. If his face lights up at the mere mention of the word, then I'd be afraid, very afraid. It's just not natural. Some men fear that they'll never be able to

Fig. 2.3 "Oh mommy, I mean Mandy, I do love you." An unusual keenness for marriage may mean that he wants you to be his replacement mother.

watch a football game again once they tie the knot, and sadly, around 80 percent of them are right. Others can't wait to move out from their parents' house and get themselves a replacement mother who'll carry on the cleaning, cooking, and nurturing duties. What you want is a "maybe, but not for a while," because men are so vague that a while could mean anything from 10 minutes to 10 years.

When you ask him when he'll call

(Fig. 2.4) A nasty one, this. How does he know? He could get hit by a bus or meet someone nicer than you. He might lose your number, except that's rubbish. If he likes you, he'll write it down on 256 bits of paper just in case he misplaces one. Don't ask men when they're going to call. They do not have built-in organisation systems that can think further ahead than the next drink or the next issue of *Maxim*. Which is fair enough. If he says, "Tomorrow," and then he doesn't call because he fell asleep or forgot, you'll be suicidal. If he says, "I don't know, because it doesn't matter," he's being too honest for his own good.

Fig. 2.4 He knows what it is, he just won't pick it up.

BODY LANGUAGE

Being able to read body language is a useful skill; more so than knitting or speed walking, for instance. Why? Because unlike the other two, it tells you loads about a man without him even realising that he's giving away his deepest thoughts and feelings with every pose and gesture. So, how can you tell whether he's interested in you or about to call security to have you removed? If he's . . .

Folding his arms across his body

(Fig. 2.5) This isn't a great sign, but it is a sign of many things. He may have developed hideous sweat patches under his arms. He may have a button missing (the horror!) from his shirt. He may be wearing a bullet-proof jacket and not want you to notice. He may be wearing a straitjacket—have you looked closely at him? Is it orange, with ties on the side? If it is, that's why. The most common reason for folding the arms across the body is as a form of defense. Not as

Fig. 2.5
He's really not
interested. At all.
Take the hint and
cut your losses
while you still
have a shred of
self-respect.

Fig. 2.6 Aagh! The most ghastly of seated positions.
Avert your gaze from the ankles at once.

in a form of defense used in a war, but one used when it comes to the opposite sex. It's a way of saying he's not interested, that he's closing himself off from you. If this news makes you cross, at least you will have a head start at getting a punch in if he has to unfold himself first.

Crossing his legs away from you

(Fig. 2.6) Any man who crosses his legs has to be a bit suspect anyway. If he's well packed in the trouser department, he shouldn't be able to cross them; there should be something in the way that makes it too uncomfortable. At least, that's my opinion. If it's not something sturdy in his pants, then it should be something sturdy in his pocket. Not a gun, but a well-stacked wallet. It also shortens the trouser, which then puts the ankles on show (see "Novelty socks" on page 10). It's a clumsy, untidy way to sit—not so bad on a sofa, but nothing short of hazardous on a bar stool. Crossing the legs and pointing them away from you couldn't be a worse sign, to be honest. He may as well just come out with it and say, "Leave me alone, woman!"

Fig. 2.7 A gesture like this means he's probably thinking, "Hmm, handsome chap, aren't I? She's one lucky lady."

Smoothing his hair or rubbing his chin

(Fig. 2.7) It depends on how he's touching himself, so to speak. A gentle sweep of the palm over the hair is just to check that he hasn't had a slight electric shock during the last five minutes. A little rub of the chin suggests he's thinking about approaching you, or else he's having a reaction to his aftershave. If you notice a rash, it's the second. If not, he likes you. Or he likes someone. Maybe himself. He's nervous, and trying to smooth his hair or touch his face is a way of preening himself without actually standing up and checking himself in the mirror. If, however, you are sitting in front of a mirror, then that's exactly what he's doing. Adjusting his collar, his tie, or even spinning round his baseball cap are all the actions of a male who wants you to pay attention to him. Imagine how David Copperfield seduced Claudia Schiffer, though. Bet he grew doves out of his nostrils.

Looking over your shoulder as you talk

He's more interested in who he *could* be talking to than who he actually *is* talking to. Perhaps he's worried about being caught out talking to a woman other than his wife or his girl-friend. Maybe he's had a fling with the barmaid or even barman. Whatever the reason for the distant stare, he's keeping more of an eye on who walks through the door than he is on you. Perhaps he's even waiting to be arrested. You never know (though a burlap sack with the word "Swag" on it in big letters and $20 bills coming out of it would be a good sign). The likelihood is that if he can't con-centrate on what you're saying when you first meet, it's only going to get worse six months down the line. Fidgeting, too, whether it be changing position or fiddling around with his clothes (including his fly, although that's fairly worrying on it's own) are all signs that he's uncomfortable with the situ-ation, or possibly just has scabies. Get out while you can.

Mirroring your body language

Body language experts, who do nothing all day but stare at people's limbs, often say that mirroring each other's actions is a form of flattery. Programmes showing people on dates always go on about "How Geoff is mimicking Sandra's body language by going cross-eyed whenever she does." This is good news for you (not the cross-eyed bit, the mir-roring of other gestures). He may be a practising mime artist, or even mentally disturbed (hang on, aren't they the same thing?), but if you've tilted your head to one side and he does the same, or you lean on your elbows across the table and he does the same, then the chances are that his actions aren't conscious—although hopefully he is. This bodes well for you, as mirroring your gestures is a sure sign that he's interested. Not as sure as asking you out, but a good sign all the same. Let him buy you a cocktail and some peanuts to celebrate his interest. Worry if he mirrors you to the point that he also drinks a pink cocktail with an umbrella in it and has a high-pitched giggle.

WHO HE'S WITH

A man in a pub on his own always cuts a solemn figure. Old men always seem to drink alone in shady looking bars, as do recently divorced men who've been divorced because they're always drinking in shady looking bars. But what if this male is actually at a table, knocking back a pint, talking to someone else? What does it mean if he's . . .

Alone

(Fig. 2.8) This isn't necessarily a bad thing, although it might be. Hard to say. If he's sobbing into a whisky, it's probably a good thing for you, as he's either just been dumped or just been fired, so he'll need cheering up. Either that or he's just been declared bankrupt, or he's just found out that he's not as tall as he thought he was. If he's happily sipping on a pint, reading a book or a newspaper, or look-

Fig. 2.8 He can read! What more could
you ask for in a man?

ing at the door every time it opens, then he's probably waiting for someone. You can pounce if you so desire. For one, he can read, so that's a plus. Two, he has enough money to buy a drink, even if it's just one. Three, he might not be waiting for a woman, at least not one he knows very well, or he'd have probably already gotten her a drink. Clever, huh? If you make eye contact and he smiles, he's either polite or interested; more eye contact and another smile within a couple of minutes means he's interested. Don't mistake a nervous twitch for a smile, though. Smile back if the mood takes you and maybe he'll motion for you to join him. At least if you get it horribly wrong and approach him and he says, "I'm waiting for my wife/boyfriend," nobody but you and him will remember.

With another male of similar appearance

Men do tend to hunt in packs, and it is quite often the case that there are very similar characteristics within each group. They are probably interested in the same things, so if it's skateboarding, football, heavy metal, rock 'n' roll, or pulling the legs off small animals, they're bound to be of almost identical appearance. It's not often you see totally different hairstyles and clothes within a pack—unless, of course, they all have really weird jobs which need hats and uniforms. Then they'll just probably look like they're about to do the "YMCA." So, it could be his best buddy, a work colleague, his brother, or, worst-case scenario, his boyfriend. The body language should clear up the last one (openly kissing or holding hands would be a giveaway, pretty much). It could mean he's a nice chap, in that he's got a close friend and doesn't feel the need to be part of a big group. Maybe he's helping him with his problems, or vice versa. Unless you hear the words "I've always thought of myself as female," chances are he's just catching up with a friend. Just beware—there's only one of you, so don't encroach on their cosy chat. Let them/him come to you.

With a woman

Right, is she better looking than you? If she is, you'll automatically think it's his girlfriend. If she's not, you'll have her down as his sister, which she may well be, but only if it's a film. You know the classic, "But I thought you were cheating on me with that beautiful woman!" "What? That was my sister!" It's generally a load of old rubbish, but if they're just chatting and there's no physical contact, or if the contact is just a hand on the shoulder as he gets up to get her a drink, then it's nothing. If he's got his hand halfway up her skirt, I would hope it's his wife/girlfriend. If they're sitting in the corner, it might even be someone else's wife/girlfriend. Best to leave this one, because unless the woman comes over and says, "My brother would like to take you out for dinner," you may well cause trouble even just smiling at him. Some women are wrong in the head and will throw beer on you just for looking. However, if she goes to the bathroom, by all means pass him your number, then leave in case he gets a kick out of telling her. If it were his mother, somewhere along the line she'd have spat on a tissue and wiped something off his face, smoothed down his hair, and kissed him on his forehead. Oh, and given him a box of homemade cookies.

Within a pack of males

(Fig. 2.9) The worst scenario of all, if you're interested in him. For him to break from the pack and go it alone, even if you are just three feet away, is akin to a soldier deserting his troops mid-fire. If his approach fails, they'll never let him forget it. If his approach wins, they'll never let either of you forget it. If he doesn't do anything about it, ditto. Men in packs are like vultures–they'll probably all want a pound of flesh, but only one will be strong enough to push his way to the front and succeed. There's always the risk that it could be set up, and that if he asks you if he could buy you a drink and you say "Yes," he'll punch the air and shout, "Ha, you suckers! Show me the money!" and then walk back over to

Fig. 2.9 Men hunting in packs. "Yeah, ten bucks to land
that dog in the red top."

them whilst doing that kind of circular dance thing with his
arms that immature men in bad comedies do when they win
stuff or kiss a girl. Packs of men are dangerous, and should
be always be approached with caution and a bucket load of
confidence. You'll probably scare the pants off them if you
go within six feet. Once one of them runs, they'll all follow.

With an older looking man

Is he a rent boy or is it his dad? Squint and imagine him
with grey hair–if he looks like the man he's talking to, it
might be his dad. If he writes him out a check, it could still
be his dad loaning him money to pay the gas bill . . . but it
could also mean he's not his dad, and he's paying him for
something entirely different. Then again, it could be his
boss. Or the CIA, quizzing him over something sinister.
How to tell for definite? If it's his boss, he'll shake his hand
when he leaves. If it's his dad, he'll shake his hand and give
him a hug. If it's neither, he'll just leave. If it's the Secret
Service and he's guilty, they'll leave together. With some
handcuffs. Of course, you can only speculate from a
distance, but if he makes eye contact with you and smiles,
it's unlikely that he's with his sugar daddy. Unlikely . . . but
not impossible!

HOW HE GETS AROUND

When you imagine a man coming to pick you up for a date, my guess is he's in an Aston Martin, not on a tandem. A man's transport is an extension of his habitat as well as his personality. Look and learn, ladies, look and learn. If he turns up . . .

On a motorised scooter or skateboard

Oh dear. This is bad. Here's a man who repeats the mantra "You're as young as you feel" instead of the more sensible "You're as young as you are, and you're not 11 years old." Who wants to date a man who pushes himself to work with his foot? Is he going to bring another skateboard along for you when you go out? Would you want to date a man in the first place who wears jeans that end before his leg does? Of course not. What he lacks in parking tickets and traffic jams he makes up for in embarrassment. He'll spend all his money on skate magazines, wheel nuts, and bandages for when he comes off and scrapes his knee caps. Not good. You'll spend most of your time in the emergency room explaining that he's your boyfriend, not your son.

By bicycle

(Fig. 2.10) Either he's deeply passionate about the environment and doesn't wish to contribute to pollution levels, or he simply never learned to drive. Was it because he was too lazy, too poor, or grounded at the time that all his friends got cars?

Fig. 2.10 "Fancy a lift, love?"
Er, how exactly?

You'll never know unless you take the risk of talking to him, and then you might get in trouble for wearing leather shoes or not recycling your chewing gum. A rusty old bike is bad enough, but serious cyclists should be avoided at all costs–anyone who wears a pointy helmet, tight Lycra shorts, and a yellow vest really isn't capable of being sexy. Plus, sweat between the legs and seat pressure add up to infertility. Go out with him and it'll probably lead to infidelity, too.

In a chauffeur-driven car

Is he rich, or has he had his license revoked? How can you tell? You can't, unless the chauffeur looks like it could be his mother or younger brother. Does he not drive himself because he believes it is beneath him? Perhaps. In that case, he'll probably ask you to tie his shoelaces and wipe his backside for him. Mind you, it could go either way–he may have a housekeeper and a maid, which will mean you won't have to lift a finger, other than to point at a speck of dust they've just missed. Still, there's something not quite right about a man who has money but doesn't want to drive. He may be a raging alcoholic; then again, he may just be rich and not enjoy driving. Your call.

In a top-of-the-line sports car

Was that him? You might have found out if he hadn't been going so fast! We all know the saying that men in sports cars are making up for a lack of produce down below. I think this idea was started by a man who couldn't afford a sports car, in the hope that women would think it true and date the poorer man instead. Rubbish. A sports car says, "Hang on to your hat, lady, you're in for a thrill," and I for one wouldn't say no to that. It will play havoc with your hair if it's a convertible, but you'll get an instant face-lift as you pull away from the traffic lights. A nice car really says, "I've got a nice car," and also spells out quite clearly that he has no intention of settling down and having kids just yet. It's a two-seater for a reason, honey.

On a motorbike

We all like to feel something throbbing between our legs–
unless it's a boil–but men and motorbikes are like women
and cats; their bike is their baby, their one true love, and woe
betide any woman who tries to get in the middle. Choosing
a bike over a car is his way of saying, "Leave me alone." He's
independent, knows his own mind, has a wardrobe full of
leather, and probably likes a good argument, as it's an
excuse to go out for a ride and "let off steam." He'll be quite
minimalist, unless he's on a Harley Davidson with its daft
saddle bags for sandwiches and chips, but this isn't always a
good thing. I mean, how's he going to bring you a bunch of
flowers on a motorbike? He'll also have sweaty hair, unless
he's Tom Cruise in *Top Gun*. And he's not.

In a helicopter

Is it Donald Trump? Quite possibly. If it isn't, he probably
wants to be. Helicopters are no-nonsense, but can be a
problem when it comes to parking. He'll leave a terrible
patch on your front lawn and probably take off the top of
the bushes, not to mention your hair. It's all very well pop-
ping out to the supermarket in a helicopter to save time, but
it's not that practical. Here's a man who can't wait for anything, other than to get a pilot's licence, so it's unlikely he'll
wait long enough for you to do your hair or make-up or
decide what pair of shoes to wear. He'll have good vision
and probably be clued in about things like weather forecasts
and the price of aviation fuel, so he could prove useful for
that, if not for the fact that *he's got a helicopter*, which is a good
enough reason to be interested in him.

HIS NATURAL
HABITAT

LIVING ROOM

A man's habitat says all there is to say about him. A quick scan of the room while he's making you the obligatory coffee that you don't even want will fill your mind with enough information to write a profile akin to something the FBI would draw up. Take note of the following . . .

The floor

It's always a good sign when you can see it, for a start, and when it's not covered in clothes, animal hair, or corpses. Obviously, if it is, leave immediately. Does he have a wooden floor? That's a good sign. It means no carpet mites, and it'll show if he's unfaithful because the other woman might leave a stiletto mark in the wood. If he regularly slides around in just his socks, it will also show that he's a lot of fun. He's probably quite style conscious, and if the floor is really clean, he's proud of his habitat and won't expect you to clean it.

The furniture

(Fig. 3.1) If there isn't any, you should be worried—the last person entertained here must have been a police officer. There's minimalist, and then there's about to be arrested, which is more like criminalist. Either that or it's being fumi-

Fig. 3.1 Nothing resembling any of these standard household items in his living room? Now is the time to start worrying. . . .

gated. It's also possible that it's not his place at all; maybe he knows a real estate agent who loaned him a key to impress you. When it comes to what you sit on, as long as it's clean and the springs aren't sticking into your back, it should do. Anything other than that is a bonus when it comes to the male habitat. Leather suggests he's pretty sexual (it is wipe-clean after all); something flowery from the '80s says he doesn't care. Fish around for loose change down the sides if it's a horrid sofa—you might need it for a taxi.

The décor

(Fig. 3.2) Wallpaper or exposed bricks? Curtains or blinds? Cushions or, uh, no cushions? Men who inhabit places with exposed brickwork fall into two categories: the first are those who are rich and stylish, with bricks that have been treated, painted white, and look lovely. The second are those who have watched too many home-improvement programmes, got a bit too curious, and removed half the wall without thinking. Outdated wallpaper is inexcusable, as paint has been available for many years now. If he rents, it's not his fault, but if he owns the place and it looks like crap, that's probably how it's going to look forever, unless you're handy with a paintbrush.

There's cool retro, like 1960s or 1970s design, and lamps, furniture, and the odd orna-ment shows he's thought about it. But if only the wall-paper and curtains are old, and bad old, then he's not thought about it at all.

Fig. 3.2 There's good retro, and then there's bad retro. In case you were wondering, this is a prime example of bad retro.

Fig. 3.3 If you spot a Mariah Carey album or Engelbert Humperdinck's Greatest Hits amongst his CD collection, panic.

His record collection

(Fig. 3.3) This is most men's pride and joy. They'll have started it off when they were 10 years old with a novelty Christmas song or something by the Clash or Sex Pistols. Which, in actual fact, belonged to their older brother. Anything embarrassing should be hidden away; if it's on display, then he's not embarrassed. "Flashdance" is not a title you'd want to see in any straight man's stack of wax; neither is anything by Judy Garland, Barbra Streisand, or Mariah Carey. Acceptable embarrassments include Bon Jovi, AC/DC, and Whitney Houston, unless they look brand new. A succession of compilation albums or vastly different types of music (tribal and Dean Martin, anyone?) show he's either schizophrenic or simply not passionate about anything in particular, which could also stretch to his women. Ouch. If all his records or CDs are lined up in alphabetical order, then depending on your level or organisational skills, this could be a winner. It certainly works for me, even though I don't manage it with my own CDs.

His books and magazines

(Fig. 3.4) Women are always told to hide self-help books when men visit their apartment. That is sensible advice, as any woman displaying titles such as *I Am Desperate to Get Married* or *Men Are Evil and Are at Fault for Everything* would frighten off the keenest of admirers. Men don't tend to go for self-help books, believing, of course, that they don't need

Fig. 3.4 Suitable titles for a male's bookshelf include those on war, crime, and alcohol, but not books about steam trains.

any advice from anyone and would only use it to prop up a wonky table anyway. This is a total lie. They'll have books telling them how to pleasure a woman (give her your credit card?), how to make spaghetti and meatballs, and how to get rich quick, but they'll all be "hidden" under the bed. Books on war, cars, and survival techniques are standard issue. As for magazines, soft porn shows he's interested but not weird, and anything on custom-made cars, dangerous motorcycles, or sports are fine. Anything to do with steam trains or trout, however, should count against him.

Pictures

I once dated a man who had nothing on his walls other than white paint and an empty bulletin board. Well, it had pins on it, but that was it. No photos, no pictures. Thankfully there were no rugs brought back from his travels either, but a vast amount of white space does nothing but unnerve me. He said it was because he hated clutter; I think it was because he hated the world. OK, so there's nothing worse than a living room full to bursting with Victoriana, but it's a bit odd if there are no photographs of his family, or even someone else's family. No art on the walls? Weird. How are you supposed to work him out if there are no clues? It could be the other way round, though, with the classics prevailing—Van Gogh's horrible *Sunflowers*, that *Scream* painting, and so on. All that shows is a lack of imagination, which is worse than a lack of pictures in the first place.

HIS BEDROOM

Not so long ago he'd be hiding anything other than his socks from his mother; now he's got girlfriends to hide things from. Whatever he's panicked about will be under the bed. My advice—don't look. Instead, concentrate on . . .

His bed

(Fig. 3.5) Otherwise referred to as his "nest," it's likely he spends as much time awake in it as he does asleep. His nocturnal habits will be quite basic—sex, either with himself or, if he's lucky, another person, and sleep. On the weekend he may be partial to sleeping in with nothing but an egg sandwich and a "special" magazine for company. If the bed is made, the covers appear to be free of stains or animal hair, and it doesn't look like there's anything to be afraid of, either he's clean and tidy, or he's got another woman and doesn't spend much time at home. If you get a chance, look at the pillows. Any random long blonde hairs despite him having a close crop? That could spell trouble, unless he's got an Afghan hound. As for the covers, are they nice or nasty? I once dated a man with fake satin sheets, leopard print on top, zebra print underneath. I say dated: I stayed there once.

Fig. 3.5 An unmade bed is acceptable; a dirty bed—made or otherwise—is not.

You don't want to become a fire hazard while you sleep, nor feel compelled to have wild and crazy sex just because he likes animal prints. And two different prints on the same bed? As if one isn't vile enough! A well-worn teddy bear sitting on a pillow is quite sweet, but if he introduces you, run a mile. His is the domain of mad women.

His bedside table

(Fig. 3.6) Be alert. One scan of this baby and you've got his number. What you'd hope to find are reading glasses. That shows that although he can't read without them, at least he *does* read with them, and unless they're next to a book entitled *Women: How to Treat Them Like Dirt and Get Away With It*, you can relax. A hand-held game console shows he either has trouble sleeping and uses it for medicinal reasons, or he's addicted to it and would rather have his fingers running wildly over that than over your body. Chewing gum next to the bed suggests he may be too lazy to clean his teeth; a packet of condoms shows he's sensible, prepared, and mature, but also fairly presumptuous. Anything sinister like books on serial killers' methods or syringes and burnt tin foil should be noted under "not good."

Fig. 3.6 Glasses, a games console, and condoms (as long as they're less than six months old)—essential items for a sensible man's bedside table, although not necessarily in that order . . .

47

His closet

(Fig. 3.7) Has he got one, or has he just got a wonky clothes rail or one of those portable pretend closets with a zip-up plastic door? If that's the case, either he's not that fussy about his things or he's always moving. If his habitat is for-ever changing, he could well be on the run, or just unable to commit to a job, woman, or even four walls. If there is something resembling a closet, have a quick peek inside. If a corpse doesn't fall out, you're halfway there. Colour-coded clothes hanging is wrong, and has no place in a normal person's bedroom. It just means they've too much time on their hands. If all his shirts are hanging up and look ironed, then either he's very organised and does his own ironing as soon as his laundry is dry, or he's got the funds to get someone else to do it. Needless to say, it's not good news either way if there are women's clothes in there. If he catches you looking and says, "I can explain; they're not mine," then that's not good, and if he says, "Wait, I can explain; they are mine," then that's even worse. Stilettos in

Fig. 3.7 Not ironed and in no particular colour order—the man who owns this wardrobe is normal. Rejoice!

a size 12 are also bad news. Acceptable items found hanging on a hook on the inside of the door include ties (not novelty ones), spare shoelaces, a scarf, or keys. Unacceptable items are those such as fur stoles, meat, and a big chain with a padlock on it. Eerie.

Wastepaper basket

(Fig. 3.8) As dull as this may sound, you'd be a fool not to have a peep in here. Don't tip it upside down, though—people only do that in films when they're looking for an important receipt. You have no idea what might be stuck to the bottom of it, so play it safe. Come to think of it, the fact that he might have been playing it safe with someone else could be given away at this moment. Unless he's really disgusting and just throws everything on the floor by the bed, then pushes it under the rug before you come over, a healthy man's bedroom waste should include crispy toilet tissue (think about it), an empty container of hair wax or stick of deodorant, and the odd gum wrapper from when he's emptied out his pockets. If you spot an empty tub of Vaseline, anything with blood on it (unless he's already confessed to being prone to nosebleeds, which in itself is

gross enough), or anything that looks like a meat product (salami left to rot in the bedroom—nice!), then it's probably all quite normal. Obviously be outraged if he's got paper in there that could have been recycled. He's clearly determined to destroy the planet.

Fig. 3.8 The wastepaper basket. If it moves of its own accord, don't touch it.

THE KITCHEN

Kitchens harbour germs and secrets, not necessarily in that order. There are types of friendly bacteria around, but they're not usually found amongst a pile of dirty dishes. If he's invited you in "for a coffee," has he actually got any? Check out the following . . .

As you walk in

(Fig. 3.9) Is that the pungent odour of rotting vegetables? Or worse, the pungent odour of rotting takeout remains? At least a rotting vegetable offers some comfort–only because it means he's thought to buy a vegetable in the first place. For many men, their idea of eating a meal with meat and two vegetables is a burger with a sliver of pickle and a lettuce leaf. A garbage bag on the floor means either he's too lazy to get a proper trash can or he's the other way–organised enough to know the garbage has to go out that night. If there's a ring of something vile around the bag, then it's been

Fig. 3.9 The full-to-bursting black trash bag and used takeout cartons. A dangerous combination if left in the wrong hands.

there for a while and he clearly has no intentions of doing anything about it; likewise, if the bag moves and squeaks, you're in trouble. If you spot a radio in the kitchen, it's a sign that he's in there long enough to get bored—which means he is either a really good cook or a really bad one. Saucepans hanging from the ceiling, unless on bits of old string, are a sure sign that he takes his food seriously. A litter box on the floor means either he has no bathroom or he's got a cat. If it's clean, either the cat's been missing for some time, or he's so hygienic that the cat's "output" is long gone before it has a chance to settle into the litter. Such a high standard of care for his cat indicates that he'll be on hand with a drink for you when you're thirsty.

The sink and work surfaces

(Fig. 3.10) Are there plates stacked higher and more precariously than the leaning tower of Pisa? When he says, "Want a cup of tea?" would you rather cut off your own hands than drink from one of his mugs? Are there, in fact, any mugs in the kitchen? Maybe they're all under his bed, in the living room, or have walked down to the garbage dump themselves in the middle of the night. If he smokes, does he empty the ashtrays, or are there so many cigarette butts piled up in them that they look like they should be entered for a work of art? Does he have any appliances, such as a blender, coffee maker, juicer, or even a cutting board? If he's got knives hanging up on a

Fig. 3.10 Ugh! An inexcusable, revolting mass of filth. If he lets his sink get like this, just imagine the state of his underpants!

magnetic strip, he's a cook. Nobody buys proper chef's knives unless they're going to use them . . . hopefully to make dinner, that is. Is it a kitchen completely bereft of anything? Does it look like a show home? If so, he's either really, really good at this cleaning lark or he simply doesn't do any cooking. At all. Maybe he doesn't even live there. You might want to ask him about that.

The fridge door

(Fig. 3.11) The fridge door is a big thing, even if it's a small fridge. Is there a freezer? Does it have an icemaker? Because you'll want ice with your vodka late at night, so take note. Is it covered in photos of people you don't know with suntans and cocktails? Then he has friends, which is healthy. Is he in any of the photos? No? Then maybe they're someone else's friends, which is not so healthy. Ask him where they were taken and you'll instantly know if you've got someone who's "found himself" in Europe during a semester abroad,

Fig. 3.11 Alphabet magnets are great for making rude words. Just be sure they're not there to teach him how to spell.

or someone who flies by the seat of his pants ("That one was in Vegas; I needed to get out of the house for a weekend"). Are there little notes pinned up with novelty magnets? Magnets aren't a bad thing if they're retro pin-up girl ones, or cocktail, ice cream sundae, or burger ones. Even alphabet ones are cool because you can write rude words with them. Magnets to be afraid of include horrendous chauvinistic "joke" ones such as "I didn't buy my wife a fancy watch for her birthday—she's already got a timer on the oven!" What do the notes say? Anything along the lines of "Remember to get Billy's vaccinations done/pick him up from school/organise his fifth birthday party" screams single parent who has hidden all his child's things away. A note in girly handwriting saying, "I love you, lamb chop, see you at 5 p.m.!" is exactly what you think it is. Escape.

Recipe books

Everyone has at least one recipe book. It doesn't mean that it gets used for anything other than to collect dust, but we've all got one. What kind of recipe book does he have? *Five-Minute Meals for One* suggests his mom bought it for him when he left home in the hope that he would eat something other than pizza. It's practical, but kind of sad all the same. Committing to a purchase with a definite "You live on your own" makes a statement, and not one that says, "I intend to be wed before the year is out." Something ridiculous, like *The Art of Cordon Bleu 10-Course Cooking*, means he's ambitious, but if it's covered in dust rather than well thumbed, it means he's all talk and no action. A book written by a celebrity chef is a gift from a former girlfriend or sister; anything based on one dish, such as noodles, means he went on vacation and had a great meal and swore he'd only eat one staple food for the rest of his life. Of course, it's more likely that he just ended up spending more money at the local Chinese or Thai takeout, because food never tastes as good when it's home-cooked and you've had to slave over it for an hour.

THE BATHROOM

Potentially the most offensive room of all, the bathroom really does say everything about a man. Clean bath? Clean man. Dirty bath? Dirty man. It's simple. Unless, of course, the bath is only clean because he's never sat in it. A minefield of information, here are some clues as to what gives . . .

As you walk in

What does it smell like? Death? Or a summer meadow? Somewhere in between, most likely, unless he's got a cleaner. Death signals bacteria, damp, fungus, and, uh, death itself. It could be a rat, it could be a cat, it could be a former girlfriend, but it's probably just the bath mat. Pray hard that he doesn't have one of those hideous furry toilet seat covers or one around the base of the toilet. They're just put there for men to urinate on. They soak up the stench and release it through the (stagnant) air on a daily basis. Nice. Quite possibly the most hazardous item of all, aside from the shower curtain. If this is white with green dots, it's more than likely that the dots are, in fact, mold. If you take a shower there, it will stick to your legs and shoulders and become entwined in your hair. Gross. Novelty toilet seats show a man who's wasted his money, not to mention his time screwing the thing on. He's so dull you need to compliment him on his toilet seat? Freak. Piles of men's magazines beside the toilet indicate that he spends far too much time in there—he would probably count it as a hobby.

On the shelves

(Fig. 3.12) Now, a nice stock of basic toiletries is what you want here, with a mirror that he'd use to shave in front of, and a few bottles of useful stuff such as moisturiser, face wash, and aftershave. Nothing wrong with that. A bit of hair

wax, styling gel, maybe even a
comb or two. What you don't
want to see are suggestions that
he has more products, and more
need for products, than you.
Anything designed for men is
OK, as long as it doesn't say
"Anti-Aging" or "This Will Give
You Hair, Baldie!" because you
have enough insecurities of your
own to put on him, never mind
him agreeing with you when you

Fig. 3.12 For essential
grooming: a mirror.

talk about crow's feet and fine lines. Any syringes saying
"Botox" on the side should be noted. A clean electric razor
or a rust-free wet-shave razor that doesn't look clogged with
stubble is to be expected, but a straight razor is a bonus if
you like your man old fashioned and ruthless. "I could cut
myself a bit, or a lot!" is his motto. Usually found next to a
white towel covered in blood.

In the cabinet

Eek! Please, don't go in there. You'll find things you didn't
even know existed, or at least hadn't seen since you looked
in your parents' cabinet when you were a child and stood
puzzled by the words "for rectal use only." Here is where
he'll have his pain killers, bandages, antiseptic lotions, and
prescription tablets, which will tell you everything you need
to know. Diazepam? Could be mild depression, insomnia,
or a stiff neck. Prozac? Uh-oh. Really strong painkillers?
He's got either a recurring injury or an addiction. Or an
addiction to recurring injuries, which is even more worrying
than an addiction to pills. Rows and rows of tablets that
you've never heard of show that he's either a thief, a
hypochondriac, or very, very ill. If there are contraceptive
pills in there, then he's not telling you something—that
something being that either he's a woman, or he's already
got a girlfriend. Perhaps if you confronted him he'd tell you

they were his ex-girlfriend's and he'd been taking them for the occasional headache, which means that's all she left at his place and he's keeping them as a souvenir, and to prove that he did, at one point, have regular sex with someone other than himself. Wart remover, fungal sprays, hemorrhoid creams, and lubricating gel are all sort of normal–but you probably won't be able to withstand the shock of seeing all of them in one cabinet. Worry.

The bath

Can you see it? OK, good. Can you see what colour it is? Kind of beige/grey? Are you sure? Take a closer look. It used to be white, didn't it? Oh dear. And what's that ring around it? Dirt, that's what. And dead skin. And old soap residue. Hang on, can you see any soap? There it is: by the drain, covered in hair. And there's no plug, it's just a hole. That's pretty scary. No bath plug? No bath. If there's a damp washcloth draped over the side, it will explain any foul stench. Shampoo should be evident–a bottle of dish soap or dishwasher detergent is not a sign of good grooming. A bristle brush hanging up shows he cares about his skin, just plain bristles in the bath itself shows he shaves his legs, or worse, his back, whilst sitting in water. A gleaming bath with a nice bar of hair-free soap and a brand of shampoo that you have actually heard of says, "I'm clean; touch me!" so do. A rare creature among this species, you must make the most of him.

SECTION FOUR

HIS FEEDING
HABITS

WHAT HE EATS

You can tell a lot about a man by what he eats, if only to say, "He's a lazy slob" or "He has an eating disorder." But that's pretty much all you need to know, because in the middle of the spectrum it just gets complicated. Invite yourself over for dinner and take your notebook. If he goes for . . .

Home-cooked meals

(Fig. 4.1) Does he go for traditional, staple dinners such as spaghetti bolognese, fish pie, chicken casserole, and roast beef? If he can cook them himself, he's probably got a very good relationship with his mother, who's obviously clued-up enough to have taught her son how to cook so his future wife doesn't feel as though she's married a caveman. If you ask him what his favourite dinner is and he says, "My mom's roast chicken," then you know you're in for a rough ride. If you can't cook, he'll tell his mom and she'll think you're rubbish, which is fair enough. If you can, he'll say, "Mmm, this is nice . . . but my mom makes it with fresh basil/sun-dried tomatoes/thicker gravy." You'll never win. He probably had big family meals at home where the emphasis was placed on spending quality time together. This means he's either gearing up to have eight kids with some lucky lady or he's waiting for someone to replace his mother, but not be as good as her. You have been warned!

Convenience food

(Fig. 4.2) Is he so busy that he hasn't got time to stir-fry a bit of chicken and boil some rice himself? Does he use his oven to store saucepans he has no intention of ever using, or worse, to store porn or running shoes? Who in their right mind, other than a lazy man, peels a foil lid off a plastic cup, pours boiling water inside, waits two minutes for the dust to

Fig. 4.1 He may well own a cooker, but does he know what it's for?

Fig. 4.2 A microwave—the best friend and most used appliance of Convenience Food Man.

Fig. 4.3 Magic. Takeout Man simply picks up the phone and food arrives!

grow into lumps, and then eats it and actually enjoys it? I don't understand it. Not enjoying proper food is like not bothering to wear proper clothes or have a proper bath. It reeks of ineptitude and immaturity. Every grown man should be able to cook one meal from scratch, even if it is only a fried breakfast. Or grilled breakfast. Or even boiled breakfast. Just something. In films, James Bond would bring in freshly made pancakes with strawberries, cream, and Champagne for breakfast while the lady sat on the mink duvet in her negligee worrying about nothing other than how her hair looked. These days you'll be lucky if you get a lukewarm slice of buttered toast in your lap. A waste and a mistake.

Takeout

(Fig. 4.3) OK, so he's interested enough in food to look at a menu and make a phone call, and possibly even get up out of the chair to open the door and bring it back in the living room. But is it anything nice and healthy? Is it heck. Chinese, hamburgers, pizza . . . they're all the classic "How did I get so fat?" takeout dinners. They scream of an addiction to monosodium glutamate, and he may well have an orange glow about him that doesn't come from a bottle of fake tan. A few years ago it was impossible to order in healthy food. Now you see people turning up on mopeds delivering sushi, for goodness' sake. If he makes ordering takeout a regular thing, then he's even lazier and dumber with money than Convenience Food Man. If you lived together, you'd both watch TV and eat food colourings and additives for the rest of your life, and get so fat you can't leave the house in the first place, thereby rendering you incapable of doing anything other than ordering more takeout. Dangerous.

Fast food

(Fig. 4.4) This is worse than convenience food and takeout put together. It means he can't even be bothered to put anything on a plate, put the trash in the can or even work out whether or not he can use chopsticks for his noodles. If he could, he'd just have an injection of fat; animal's knuckles, ears, and lips; more fat; and some flavourings jabbed into his backside once a week to save him the bother of chewing. One day these places will feed you as well so that you can expel even less energy and therefore get even fatter and

Fig. 4.4 It's cheap and plentiful, but fast food doesn't go so fast when it's clogging his colon.

have a heart attack while you're still in the car. Food and cars do not go. You can guarantee getting your new heels stuck in a piece of old burger, or sitting down in your new jeans on top of a bit of relish which has been stuck to the seat for five years. It shows a total disregard for his health, which means he'd make a lousy husband and an even worse father. He'll burp too much, fart too much, and he'll be so busy trying to decide whether six chicken wings and fries are a better value than a cheeseburger, fries, and onion rings that he won't be able to remember your name.

Vegan or organic

(Fig. 4.5) You have to worry about a man who doesn't feel the need for a big juicy steak, plump fried shrimp, or even a cheese sandwich. I wouldn't touch him with a 10-foot pole. You'll have to explain to him why you wear leather shoes instead of ones made from potato skins. You'll have to bring up your kids to be really pale, wondering why the other kids think they're weird because they cry when they see an egg or a gallon of milk. It's just not right. Men should have big arms, and big arms are made from beef. You don't want a man who won't make you a cup of coffee because it's freeze dried, and is therefore full of chemicals, and therefore will kill you if you so much as smell it. And don't even ask for milk with that. Soy milk is an option, but it tastes like wet cardboard. All in all, it's too much bother. Some organic things are even worse for you anyway, so tell him that. He'll spend so much on his food shopping that he won't be able to take you to the cinema. Mind you, he'd probably rather take you to a play in a tiny theatre and call it "an organic movie" instead.

Fig. 4.5 Avocados—nourishment for women and small animals, not men.

WHAT HE DRINKS

Back in the old days, real men drank ale or whisky. Nowadays, there's beer, cocktails, and even orange juice. But what does a man's drinking preference say about him? Read on and find out. If he drinks . . .

Beer

(Fig. 4.6) Hoorah, normality. But how much is considered normal? On a date with you does he drink 17 pints, or just two? Does he drink each pint within three minutes of ordering it, as if his life depended on it? This is the key, you see. There's also a big difference between drinking bottled beer and pints. Pints say, "I drink beer, and I've been doing it for ages. I can carry a pint without my arm hurting, and I don't have to go to the bar as often because there's lots of beer in one glass." Bottles say, "I like peeling off the labels if I get nervous, plus if I'm short on cash, I can spit some back in without anyone noticing." Guinness is the most macho drink of all, because it's heavier than normal pints and is a bit like drinking really cold soup. It is, as they say, a meal in a glass. It's also quite good for you within reason, so he'll be fertile and have good iron levels. He'll also probably not have room for anything to eat, so depending on how much you like your food, it could be a bad thing. You suggesting going for dinner only for him to say, "Eh? I've just had dinner. In that glass," may well be a problem, as may a rotund belly.

Juice

(Fig. 4.7) He's either driving, on a skateboard, trying to impress you in a "new man" kind of way, or he's a recovering alcoholic. Saying "Go on, just have a vodka" six times serves as a good test. If on the sixth time of prodding he

Fig. 4.6 Seventeen pints
of beer in one night is
too much.

Fig. 4.7 Orange juice—
a health-conscious male,
or the sign of a recover-
ing alcoholic?

Fig. 4.8 Spirits in a small
glass—macho enough for
detectives in films.

explodes and screams, "If I have one vodka, I'll have to have 65; I can't stop!" is a sure way of finding out. Maybe he's on antibiotics, which could spell trouble if it's something contagious. Perhaps he's detoxing. Maybe he eats badly and needs some vitamins. Perhaps he thinks all women want men to drink juice so they don't get drunk and shout at us. He might be right. It's unusual unless a man is driving, so be a bit wary. It may be that he just likes juice, but hey, he's a man, so it's not very likely. It could be the start of a downward spiral of lies. If he tells you he's a spy, he's a liar, if only for the fact that spies aren't allowed to say that they're spies. Then again he might say he's an accountant because he is actually a spy, which would also be a lie. Timid, and not likely to be very protective.

Spirits

(Fig. 4.8) This fella clearly means business. Is he in the police force? Only they always drink too much whisky in films, and it's usually kept in their desk drawer at work. Spirits without mixers say, "I'm out to get drunk," which probably isn't an attractive method of seduction.

It also means he's really hard-core, and will no doubt soon be Juice Man—The Recovering Alcoholic. Although if he drinks a lot of spirits without mixers, he may never get around to the recovering bit. If he drinks tequila or absinthe, then you've definitely got problems. He's clearly trying to kill his liver or send himself to sleep so that he doesn't have to talk to you, or worse, marry you. It also means he can't drink beer because either he doesn't like the taste, which is just weird, or because he has a small bladder. The only advantage of this is that you could end up just as drunk through kissing him, which makes it a cheap night. Spirits mixed with a soft drink gives a nice sugar high, so he's fun for about 10 minutes, but then the inevitable sugar crash brings on a headache or a moody glance in your direction for no reason other than his metabolism going crazy. Club soda is very useful for cleaning stains from walls though.

Fig. 4.9 Alco-pops are the domain of teenage girls, and are not to be consumed by men worthy of a woman's attention.

Alco-pops

(Fig. 4.9) What's wrong with a grown man drinking a drink made for girls that tastes like cough mixture, I hear you ask.

Fig. 4.10 A cocktail, sir? I don't think so! Have you ever seen James Bond twirling one of those little umbrellas?

Well, the answer is: everything. It's what the word "wrong" was invented for. I once went to a restaurant with a so-called man who ordered an orange-based alcoholic drink in a bottle. I ordered a lager. When the drinks came, they were placed in the position you would think correct–lager for man, orange drink for lady. So-called man wasn't even embarrassed by the waiter's faux pas. How can you take any man seriously when he's lifting up a bottle of bright red water containing a teaspoon of vodka and four tablespoons of additives, that requires him to lean over the bar, ask for it by name, and then say, "Ooh, I'll try the watermelon one this time." What? Is beer watermelon flavour? No, it's not. Either he hates the taste of proper alcohol, which is just plain weird, or he thinks that by getting in touch with his feminine side he will actually be more appealing. He is wrong. He will actually appear to be gay, and possibly toothless, what with all the sugar and sweeteners he's putting away.

Cocktails

(Fig. 4.10) James Bond has just had a mention, but deserves another one here. He's one hell of a classy predator. But there's drinking a martini, shaken not stirred, and then there's drinking a martini with a splash of vodka, some gin, a touch of Bailey's, a drop of lime, some crushed blackberries, a pint of rum, and three little paper umbrellas. Not so classy. An inferiority complex lies beneath the confident exterior. Compare a Long Island Iced Tea with a Cosmopolitan–a man could sit in a dark corner and just about get away with the first, but a pink drink with sugar around the edge of a dainty glass just doesn't work. Really. If you order a Cosmopolitan or a French Martini, he should order a "tall" drink from the menu, and it shouldn't be pink. Or blue. Or any colour that you would consider wearing against your skin. Rum-based cocktails in a tall glass are acceptable; watching a man drink through a straw is not.

WHEN HE FEEDS

Is he a grazer, like a cow, munching on snacks throughout the day and getting fatter by the minute, or does he get up in the middle of the night and swallow the entire contents of the fridge like some nocturnal scavenger? If he feeds . . .

At breakfast time

(Fig. 4.11) A sensible breed, this one. He's obviously had it drummed into him from a young age that breakfast is the most important meal of the day. Important because a) it provides fuel for the body to go about general duties such as hunting, gathering, and mating, and b) breakfast is still available in some establishments at lunchtime, which is cool. Pecking at some cereal that looks like little sticks is a bit of a lady habit though, so beware a man who doesn't actually relish his food. Cereal with toast or fruit shows a healthy attitude as well as appetite, so he could well be around for years. If you're looking to inherit his money via a heart

Fig. 4.11 A real man's breakfast. A real man with a short lifespan, admittedly . . .

attack, it's unlikely you'll get any joy. He'll probably go jogging afterwards. If he fills up for the day on sausage, egg, and bacon, it means he enjoys his food but knows his limits. It saves time thinking about what to eat later on, which means he's got more time to think about buying presents for you.

At lunchtime

(Fig. 4.12) Business lunches tend to go on for about five hours, which effectively takes him into the evening. The trouble is, he'll be so full, because he's eaten as much as his expense account will allow, that it's highly likely that he'll actually spend most of the evening—when he's with you—asleep. The bonus is that you don't need to cook for him; the sad fact is you'll be bored and lonely while you watch him get fat. Grabbing a sandwich and eating it at his desk whilst simultaneously answering the phone and looking at porn on the Internet means he thrives on stress. He can probably take half an hour for lunch, go for a walk, even curl up under his desk and have a sleep, but the "I haven't got time!" attitude is generally created by people who just wish they were important enough not to have the time. No lunch break equals a moody man who resents his boss, and

Fig. 4.12 "I don't have time for lunch!" Yes he does,
he just wishes he didn't.

it may mean he's too much of a wimp to stand up for himself outside of work as well. A sparrow amongst the pigeons, fighting for a crumb and some dignity.

In the evening

Some men are weird and can't be bothered to get up early enough to have breakfast, are genuinely too busy to have lunch, somehow don't pass out, and then only eat in the evening. Unfortunately, they'll have a tendency to eat too much in the evening, which results in piles of washing up and piles of flab around the tummy if he eats fairly late. Eating in the evening does mean you'll be more likely to get a restaurant date rather than a cheese sandwich, and it also makes him rather more appealing on a sociable scale. He's likely to have been brought up to eat a proper meal around the table with his family, and this points to him being a decent all round kinda guy. It's also less likely that he spends the best part of his evening in a lap-dancing club. He'll enjoy time to himself at home, which means he's pretty stable in the head and less likely to have some kind of depressive thing going on that makes him have no desire to spend any time with himself. On the other hand, he may be a serial killer or total freak who enjoys only spending time with himself, cooking up romantic dinners for two—him and his latest victim. A little over-reactive, maybe, but always a possibility. I mean, lions eat in the evening.

In the middle of the night

A prowler, adept at creeping around in the dark to find what he wants. OK, so refrigerators have a light inside them to help you decide whether you want to eat a pound of grapes or a pound of cream cheese, but this male needs to have good instincts to get around at this time of night, fill his tummy, and get back to bed without waking his dog, his mom, or his girlfriend. He may well wear slippers, which isn't good from an aesthetic point of view, but to him they serve as protection against protruding nails and chair legs which may otherwise scrape his toe. They also keep his feet warm in the kitchen. Men who eat in the middle of the night wonder why they're putting on weight. You will also wonder why he's putting on weight, as he will deny he eats anything other than "cereal, then a sandwich." Make a list of the contents of the fridge before you head for bed, then check it the next morning while he's in the shower, washing away the guilt of his midnight binge. If a carton of milk, a pack of cheese slices, and a loaf of bread are missing, you know who the culprit is. It shows an addictive personality, and a restless soul. Not good.

Throughout the day

A grazer, he eats out of boredom or insanity. He's never hungry, but never full—the worst of both worlds. Laziness contributes to this behaviour, which is not only erratic but also dangerous. We've all seen videos of grease fires on the television, or watched *ER* when someone cuts off their entire arm below the elbow with a steak knife (sometimes by accident, sometimes not), so the more visits to the kitchen, the more likely he is to injure or kill himself. Grazing shows a complete lack of time management and organisation. He's not likely to have a great job, nor a great deal of sense. You'll spend every waking moment tripping over empty milk cartons, getting potato chip wrappers stuck to your stilettos, and picking unidentifiable dried meats from the sofa. He's a weak male who can't walk past the kitchen without visiting the fridge. He'd be hopeless in a fight, as he'd be too weak to punch from never knowing the value of a square meal. It's also fairly likely that he smokes a lot of something he shouldn't. As we all know only too well, this type of male is horizontal, has few brain cells, and can't even be bothered to clean himself, never mind his apartment. Like a newborn cub, he'd eat anything you offered him if it was on a stick, in a packet, or meant he didn't have to use any cutlery.

HOW HE
OBTAINS HIS FOOD

Is he capable of providing for himself, or does his mom still cook his dinner? Can he be trusted to follow a simple shopping list? Is he a total idiot who eats the same as his cat? Read on to find out. If he eats . . .

At his mother's

Bless him. This is what you want—a man who's mature enough to fly the nest, but not so independent or macho that he doesn't go back to feed occasionally. And I do mean occasionally. Sunday lunch with his family is a real treat, and smacks of good old-fashioned family values, although if you happen to go along with him and he doesn't wash the dishes, nor clear the table, and his mother constantly questions your ability to make roast potatoes both fluffy and crispy, then maybe you've got a problem. Visiting his mother once a week for a meal is heart-warming stuff. Many folk say you can judge how a man will treat his partner by how he treats his mother and/or his sisters. What you want is a perfect balance—the son who says "yes" to seconds but not to thirds, who clears up and does the dishes, kisses his mom on the cheek, then takes you home for some

Fig. 4.13 Does he eat with these (in the correct order), or does he use his fingers?

serious lovin'. What you don't want is a lazy slob who's still tied to his mother's apron strings. If she insists on him sitting down and won't let him help clear up, you're in trouble. That's spoilt with a capital S.

At a restaurant

Now, there are two types of man when it comes to restaurant dates. Type One makes a reservation, asks for a good table, and lets you know whether he'll be wearing a suit or not. The same type will invariably recommend a dish to you, but not say, "Yeah, my last girlfriend loved the wild mushroom risotto but it made her fat." He will guide and encourage you rather than treat you like a child. He should be competent when it comes to ordering wine, and not say that it is corked when it isn't, just to sound clever. Then there's Type Two. He can't be bothered to book a table, and then acts surprised and annoyed when you're plonked by the kitchen or in a draft. He'll scan the menu, turn up his nose at everything other than steak or spaghetti, then tell you to hurry up and decide what you want. He'll click his fingers at the waiter, point at the menu instead of asking for the dish, and then say something derogatory about the waiter's hair. He'll eat his meal in three seconds flat then complain that it was rubbish, but only to you because he's too scared to complain to the chef. You'll know which type you're out with before you so much as put the food on your fork. This is where manners really come into their own.

At his friends' houses

Oh please, can he not manage to feed himself? There's nothing worse than answering the door to someone who's popped round uninvited but manages to stay half the night and, in that time, clear out your fridge and cupboards like he's spring cleaning, only there's nothing to put back once it's clean. That, and the fact that he's not cleaning it either. The kind of male who's happy to let other people do the hunting and gathering while he sits back. He's the sort of man, if you can call him that, who turns up as his friends are sitting down to dinner, prompting them to say, "Uh, we were just about to eat. But there's enough for three," even though that's a lie, because who makes dinner for three when there's two of you? Nobody, that's who. What it means is they will both eat less, which is crap. This male will become a social outcast within time, as all his friends will learn his tricks and start to pretend that they are out when they are well and truly in. Hiding behind the sofa and turning lights out quickly loses its appeal, so eventually folk will just cave in and say, "Vulture! Get your own food!"

Alone

What's wrong with him? Has he lost all his friends due to behaviour outlined above, or does his mother live too far away for him to get over there for food? Does he feel so passionate about his shopping list that if he went to the supermarket with a friend or girlfriend, they'd sabotage his plans by adding something off the list to the basket? Does he show signs of being obsessive about his shopping, like an old lady? Try taking things out from the cart when he's not looking and adding random items instead. Swap, say, a can of baked beans for some diapers. It's great fun, but it also shows you whether he'll go mad or just look a bit puzzled when he gets to the checkout. If he's puzzled, he's alright. If he goes mad, then the random items have upset his equilibrium and he may lash out at passers-by. If he eats alone as well, is it a coincidence that he's always "just eaten" when you turn up (a dirty plate in his hand on its way to the sink is a good clue, but it might be a prop—check it's not dried-on food or a picture), or is there something more sinister going on, such as bulimia or an aversion to company in general?

HIS JOB

WHAT HE DOES
FOR A LIVING

It's hard to tell what a man does for a living just by looking at him—unless, of course, he's in uniform, on the checkout at a supermarket, or at the counter in the bank. Scratch that, then, it's easy to work out what he does. But how will his job affect you? If he's . . .

A real estate agent

He spends all day lying through his teeth. "Yeah, uh, it's a cosy apartment which needs a little updating," translates as "It's a hellhole the size of a telephone booth and hasn't seen a lick of paint since 1978." So when he says to you, "You're the only one for me, baby," it might not be strictly true. He's a man who will generally get what he wants by turning on the charm; if that fails, he'll become aggressive and intimidating. His predatory nature leaves no hiding place if he wants to ensnare you. He won't just track down where you live, he'll value it while he's outside looking up at your bedroom window. Probably while he makes notes like, "Outside front wall has large crack approx. one foot long, window sills need replacing," things like that. He might use empty properties that he has on his books to lure you in—pretending an apartment in an exclusive millionaire's block is his when, in fact, he's just shown 36 people around it that morning. It's not to say that all real estate agents are liars, it's just that most of them are. They spend all day exaggerating the size of things, so what's to stop him carrying it over into his personal life? Plus, anyone who works on commission jumps up and punches the air quite a lot, so if you feel that might be slightly embarrassing, or even extremely irritating, don't even think about going out with him.

A fireman

(Fig. 5.1) What is it about fire engines that make us women go to pieces? Is it the flashing blue lights and loud sirens, meaning "Get out of the way, we need to save lives!" that makes firemen kings of the urban jungle and infinitely more attractive than other types of male? They're brave, unselfish, and can sleep on tiny beds in a room full of other men who are snoring. How clever is that? Shift work means you'll have to accommodate him, as it were, whenever he can manage to see you between fires, rescuing cats from trees, and removing toes from bath faucets. Your friends will be jealous that you're dating someone so manly and may either a) attempt to jump him, or b) never speak to you again, but that's just life. He'll smell of soot a lot of the time, but it'll just serve to remind you how brave he is. You'll need to be able to cook steak and eggs because he'll need lots of energy to slide down poles and run up crumbling stairways. He'll be fit, and have great arms. He can carry you home when you've had one too many and even get you up the stairs in one clean swoop. He'll be able to teach

you how to use a fire extinguisher as a weapon and also how to smother a grease fire without singeing your eyebrows off. There's a possibility that he may not actually be a real fireman, but just a stripper dressed as one. You'll be able to tell by the Velcro running down the front of his trousers and the portable stereo he puts down in front of you.

Fig. 5.1 A fireman—he can save you from unpleasant things like fires and bears.

A policeman

"You can't park there. That skirt's way too short. Did you copy this CD? Have you got a receipt for it? No, I didn't think so. Is that marijuana I smell?" Good grief, this could be a difficult one. If he's older than you and really into his work, it might feel like you're going to get told off all the time—probably because he tells you off all the time. You'll be terrified that he'll find out you stole a lip liner when you were 13 years old, and he'll also be adept at interrogating you if you're not in when you say you will be or if you've had a telephone call from an ex-boyfriend. If he's a detective, he'll be at work all the time, keep his curtains closed so that the living room is really dark—at least that's what detectives on cop shows normally do—and also refer to everyone as "You," as in "Yeah, I'm talkin' to you." He'll have a bottle of whisky in his desk drawer and in the toilet tank in his apartment; he'll eat junk food at night and doughnuts by day, reek of bad coffee, and smoke like a chimney. He'll have an ex-wife, money problems, and bad suits. This is, of course, speculative, but just look at *Columbo*. See? It's all true!

A construction worker

(Fig. 5.2) Now you might think you're on to a good thing here, what with construction workers generally being able to build and all. But you can forget about his nest-building talents. How many secretaries type letters when they get home from work? How many welders start joining bits of metal together after dinner? Not many, because if you've been doing something all day, chances are you don't really want to carry on when you get home. Most construction workers are notorious for starting jobs in their own homes and never getting around to finishing them. He'll rip out his kitchen one night on a whim—with his own bare hands, of course—then stand there scratching his head and looking at it for about six months. You'll ask him to put some shelves up, and he'll say yes, but never do it. Instead, he'll be prac-

Fig. 5.2 He's a construction worker, so he won't chat you up–he'll wolf whistle instead.

tising wolf whistles and getting Celtic-band tattoos that mean absolutely nothing. He'll traipse mud and plaster and bits of his bacon sandwich through your hallway. Your reward for putting up with such mess is, um, his ability to lift the sofa with one hand while you vacuum underneath it.

A commodity broker

Nice car. Nice suits. Nice cell phone. Nice personality? Who cares? No, really. It'll be more a case of "who knows?" as everything will be done with such speed and ferocity that you'll hardly have time to catch your breath.

This breed plays hard and works hard, and in between looks at cars on the Internet. All those long hours waving their arms about on the trading floor and slamming down phones to Japan at the same time as answering another 12 phones from places we've never even heard of mean he's stressed to the max and liable to burn himself out by the age of 35, if not sooner. The good news is that if you can put up with him being so highly strung, he may be able to retire within a couple of years, and then you can just go sailing all day whilst sprinkling diamonds on your cereal. A fast mover and fast talker, he could end up treating you like foreign currency: one minute you're in favour and worth your weight in gold, the next, you're a discontinued foreign coin found down the back of the sofa. Enjoy it while you can.

WHAT HE EARNS

"I don't care about money, as long as he's got a nice personality . . ." say the ladies. *Yeah, right. Funny how most women who say that are dating rich men. So what kind of life can you expect depending on his salary? If he's earning . . .*

Under $15,000

Where the hell does he work? In a time warp where they pay a dime a week? Granted, there are a lot of low-wage jobs out there, but this is the twenty-first century. Some moisturisers cost as much as that. It's unlikely that with wages of this kind he'll be able to woo you with expensive gifts, unless he's decided you're worth going bankrupt for. Maybe he's good at art, and can draw you romantic cards or paint you a dozen roses instead of forking out for the real thing–OK, so it's all he can do, but how easy is it to buy flowers in comparison to painting them? Even if he's rubbish at painting, it's still the thought that counts, unless he thought roses looked like breasts, which is often what men draw when given 10 minutes and a pencil. Maybe he's an intern or a trainee who will see his wage rise once he's experienced, in which case he could earn three times the amount. He must have patience and, unless he's riddled with debt, be adept at managing on a budget. Your grandmother would like him. If he makes soup with leftover vegetables, then you know he's in it for the long haul, and you might have to rethink your dreams of holidays in the Caribbean and long lunches at the latest celebrity haunt.

$15,000 to $35,000

This is branching out into being able to take you out to dinner, albeit maybe only one weekend in four, and buying you little gifts such as reduced-price flowers from the gas station or squashed cream cakes. If he rents a place on his own, chances are most of his wages go straight to his landlord, and on bills. You won't know whether he's simply cheap or romantic if you turn up to find the place lit by candles until you try to turn a light on. If nothing happens, he's cheap. If the room lights up, he's romantic. It's a simple and effective test, yet one which could prove quite embarrassing for him, so resist the urge until he's left the room. Continually leaving items of clothing at your place, especially if it's mostly socks and underpants, means that he doesn't own a washing machine. You're a woman, which means you'll just pick them up and wash them because that's what we're programmed to do. He'll be clever enough to leave a T-shirt sometimes so that he can say, "I thought you'd like to wear it to bed so it reminds you of me," which translates loosely as "Can you wash it for me? I can't afford a washing machine."

Fig. 5.3 Presents, or just empty boxes? It's the thought that counts, isn't it? You've got to be kidding. . . .

$35,000 to $60,000 (Fig. 5.3) This is more like it—a reasonable chunk of a wage, the top end of which gives him enough money to save up and put down a deposit on his own place. It's a decent wage that affords him such luxuries as soap, bleach, food, and electricity. He'll be able to take you to see a movie, and he may well have enough in reserve to treat you to some popcorn as well. There's no excuse not to own a car, even if he doesn't know how to drive it, and you should be taken away for the odd romantic break on holiday weekends. If he's had student debts, he'll be paying them off now, and he might use that as an excuse not to treat you to a new necklace or something fancy like that. But we all know that expensive gifts for you should be a priority, so that's clearly rubbish.

$60,000 to $100,000

(Fig. 5.4) This is a hefty enough sum to furnish his fridge with smoked salmon, cream cheese, olives, and imported beer that you can't pronounce. Expect a bottle of decent white wine to be chilling in the fridge door at all times. Birthdays should bring nice surprises like a cashmere sweater or fancy earrings (i.e., ones that won't turn your earlobes black). He can afford to get his car cleaned inside and out, so no dog hairs or fast-food wrappers stuck to your coat. If he's worked his way up to earning this amount, he's going to be seriously strung out when he realises how much he's paying in taxes. You may have to be on hand in red underwear to ease his pain. Unless he's having to work 125 hours a week to earn this much, it should mean that he gets to delegate stuff to his minions whilst surfing the Internet for vacations for the two of you. If he's separated—from a wife, not himself—then expect a whole different ball game. Once his earnings go over 25¢ an hour, she'll be on the phone demanding maintenance for the cat's dentist and the like. A double-edged sword, this one—comfortable, but not *that* comfortable.

Fig. 5.4 A non-stop supply of the finest Champagne will do nicely . . . for starters.

Millions

(Fig. 5.5) By now you're all set. No more going to work by subway or bus—how about a chauffeur-driven car or helicopter? Hang on, why are you even going to work? Aren't you having your hair done at noon, followed by a facial? Well, so is he. Chances are he's read something in a magazine that says all men should have clean nails and wash their faces, and that if they can afford it, they should go a bit further and maybe even put bath foam in with the water. Rich men who are at ease with their sexuality and even more at ease with spending money will generally be well groomed, from polished shoes to a polished face. It is possible that too much money may have turned him into a total idiot, particularly if he's past his peak. In comes the highlighted hair, cowboy boots, Harley Davidson motorbike, and 17-year-old girlfriends called Candy or Bambi. Hey, why not have both? He may treat women like dirt, because he doesn't need to work on his personality when most women simply require a heavy wallet. Then again, he might be rich and nice, donating cash to children's homes, building amusement arcades in old people's homes, and paying for abandoned animals to go on vacation—things like that. If he's a weirdo who puts it all in the bank and won't spend a penny, you'll have to marry him and kill him, simple as that.

Fig. 5.5 He'll have a terrible time trying to park, but it beats hanging about in the rain at bus stops.

HIS AMBITIONS/
ASPIRATIONS

When boys are little, they usually want to be firemen, football players, policemen, or fighter pilots. Some of them grow up to do what they intended, and some don't—they just become accountants or telemarketing executives. How can you tell if he's going to be a success at work? Is his aim . . .

Just to get to work on time

Oh dear. You've got problems if you're staying over at his place, it's 2 a.m., and he's doing saucy things to you despite your protestations that you have work in the morning, while he whispers, "I don't care, my job isn't important, I'll just stay in bed." Going back to dinosaur days, men had important jobs, like killing woolly mammoths so that the missus might make him some fetching furry pants while he fixes the tusks to the wall for hanging dead rabbits on. That's what you want, a real man, not someone who's job is so insignificant that he doesn't even have to phone in sick because they don't notice if he's there or not. It doesn't say much about what he wants out of life. This isn't so bad if he's under 25, but anything over that and the alarm bells should be ringing. If he doesn't care what he does, what he earns, or whether he's doing anything useful or worthwhile now, he never will. You'll be forever scraping by in life, the equivalent of mangy dogs pulling old bones out of trash cans. Not appealing.

To get his own assistant

(Fig. 5.6) And why would that be? So he could run a more efficient office and get home earlier to you? Unlikely. It's more a case of him wanting to exert some power in the

Fig. 5.6 "And if you could just get my wife's birthday present, pick up my dry-cleaning, and trim my nose hair, that would be great."

work place, such as "Dammit, I said I take my coffee black!" or "Ursula, I need some hard, fast cash; get me my mother on the phone, now!" He'll have watched too many James Bond films and have fantasies that every personal assistant wears her hair pinned up, gazes at her boss longingly over her spectacles, and whips off said specs, lets down her hair, and whips open her blouse at every given moment. It'd make him feel important and give him someone else to order around. He'd also be able to ask her to buy your birthday present, book tables at restaurants, and sort out his dry-cleaning. In other words, he wants a girlfriend-cum-mother who can't answer him back. And who can blame him? Just watch he doesn't practise on you. A dominant male/sub-servient female role is out-dated and shows a man with a need to show off and be in control.

To get a better company car

Ah, male pride at its best. Is he constantly whining about someone in his office having a better car than him? Does it have alloy wheels and do another two inches to the gallon more than his? Is he still at school? He may as well be. He's still that little boy who wants what the boy next door had first, be it a potato gun or a remote-control boat. If it's purely because someone else on his level has a better car, then it's purely childish. This points to a future with a man who's constantly going to whine about stuff, with the odd "It's not fair" as a bonus at the start of most conversations. If it's genuinely because he deserves a nicer car, then it's right that he should stand up for himself. It shows he's no pushover, at least, which means you're on sturdy ground for the future—although when he's rich and you ask for a better car, it might not work the same.

To run the company

(Fig. 5.7) There's nothing wrong with aspiring to be the Alpha Male, but if he says this in the interview, he's in trouble, unless the boss is his dad. Rising at the crack of dawn every day and working until midnight shows he's keen, if not crazy. However, it may all be a waste of time if it goes unnoticed. Does he complain that he's not appreciated? If so, he probably does the same about you whilst at work all those hours. If he's putting in the time and not getting any reward, however, he may go off the rails like Michael Douglas did in that film where he has a really crap day and starts killing people on his way home. If he's moving up the career ladder faster than you can say, "Did your assistant buy me these crotchless red panties? Because if that's the case, I feel a little uncomfortable in more ways than one," then his efforts are paying off and you'd do well to stick with him. He obviously knows what he wants, has a clear game plan, and sticks to it. You'll just have to take a back seat to his career until he gets what he wants. If you can put up with that, you're onto a winner.

Fig. 5.7 "Yeah, I did 145 hours unpaid overtime this week,
but I don't mind. Do you like my new suit?"

To be his own boss

A strong male stands alone and successful and lets others
come to him—a bit like an elephant with a bucketful of
bananas. Ambition is attractive, but only if it's actually
achievable. If he wants to become president but is currently
spending his days flipping burgers, then he's thinking a bit
beyond his station. If he works in a place where he is learning as he goes along and has a clear picture of his goals, then
that's pretty sensible. If he spends every evening drawing
really bad cartoons or standing in front of a mirror telling
himself jokes, convinced he's the next David Letterman,
then you have to worry. If he keeps saying things like, "If
only there were something like a fridge, only smaller," and
you find yourself saying over and over, "But there is," then
he's plain stupid, not to mention irritating. If he mentions
the words "business plan" and "capital" in the same
evening, he's talking sense. Just don't sign your apartment
over to him when you're drunk, or marry him right after he
asks you to take out life insurance.

IF HE IS UNEMPLOYED

In the 1950s, men went to work in a long coat and shiny shoes while women got the dinner on and washed the kids' faces fresh for a kiss from Daddy. And that's how it should be. Honestly. Just look what happens when tradition is abandoned. Chaos!

Is he still a student?

(Fig. 5.8) If he's pretty young, then that's OK. Maybe he's just finishing his degree and already has a job lined up. If he's at the start of one, you're going to have to be really committed to make it work. He'll have no money, but maybe he's gearing up for something worthwhile, like a career as a doctor or conservationist, or even better, a shoe designer. However, if he's just muddling his way through a degree in nothing in particular, like communications or English, then chances are he's just too scared to go to work and be an adult. He'll no doubt spend half the day in bed listening to music on his iPod, which he bought with his student loan, and only getting out of his pit for cigarettes or to pop to the corner shop for some unhealthy snacks that he can just about be bothered to eat. He will probably rent a room in a house which has horrible, dirty carpets; mismatched crockery; a dirty ring around the bath; and nothing but an out-of-date egg and a half a can of flat beer in the fridge. If he does

Fig. 5.8 Students: silly hats, no cash, and bad hygiene. Avoid.

cook, it'll be on a tight budget, so practise saying, "Mmm, that lentil sandwich is divine!" 100 times before you pop round. Expect no sense of urgency in any situation other than when he can't find the T-shirt he threw on the floor last week. The student is the weakest of the male species, other than the next one.

Is he lazy?

Ask him. "Are you too lazy to go to work?" should suffice. An answer such as "Yes" will tell you in no uncertain terms what his long-term prospects are. You can tell whether someone is lazy or just between jobs (see below) by the following: does he ever leave the house other than to collect his unemployment money? Has he ever worked a day in his life? Does he sit around writing bad television scripts or plays in the vain hope that one day he'll get published and be rich? Worse, does he not even bother doing that? Is he content with nothing but a TV and a sofa for company? Do his housemates pay all the bills and leave notes stuck to his forehead saying things like "You owe us three months' rent, you loser" while he snoozes? How will he take you out for dinner, or even for a cup of coffee, if he never works? He might be able to live off a pittance himself, but making you a daisy chain instead of buying you a Tiffany choker is only going to be sweet and romantic once, let's face it.

Is he living off his parents?

Ah, that old trick. But what kind of parents let their son live off them, like a tiny fish feeding on the underbelly of a whale? It's not normal, and it shows how little respect he has for them or himself if he's happy doing that. Maybe he's inherited a fortune, in which case that's fair enough, but even then it's hard to think much of a man who doesn't do anything with his time other than spending money on yachts and caviar just for the sake of it. Building up a business and then buying up a city is fair enough. Is he the son of somebody famous? That's entirely different. You'll get your picture in the papers as you step out of nightclubs, which is cool, but then you'll also have him moaning, "I can't be my own man because of who my father is," like a spoilt child, mainly because he is. He might be fun for a while, but he'll be so wrapped up in himself that he'll never be concerned about you. And if his mom or dad are famous-but-rubbish singers or artists who make things out of old bread and badges, you'll have to suppress your indifference constantly to appear "cool" with the fame aspect, and also to avoid saying, "Look, what they do is rubbish!"

Is he between jobs?

In most cases, this is a man's way of saying, "I'm too lazy to work but I know it makes me sound really bad." Being laid off is one thing, but if he's been sacked you need to know why. Did he have an affair with his, or someone else's, secretary? Was he stealing from petty cash or fiddling his expenses? Don't beat around the bush. If he admits that it's been a while since he worked, find out why. Perhaps he's lost confidence in himself, or maybe he's just enjoying getting up late every day. Is he having some kind of career meltdown or midlife crisis? Is it a pre-midlife crisis? Are all his friends better off financially than him? He might need a little prompting to get back to work, but you might be better off finding someone who already has a job. A man in a rut is like a dog chasing its tail–he'll go round in circles, exhaust himself, and then fall asleep. If he's keen on you, he'll probably offer to cook or clean your apartment while you're at work. If he's a nutcase, he'll rearrange your furniture and order new carpets out of boredom.

HIS MATING
HABITS

PICK-UP LINES

It's hard to walk and talk at the same time, which is why men tend to walk, then stop in front of you, then talk. But what they say is usually still rubbish if they're trying to get you back to their nest/burrow/lair. So what's his pick-up line? If it's . . .

One about eggs

You know the kind of thing. "So, how do you like your eggs in the morning? Fertilised? Ha ha ha." Or just as bad, "Go and get a quarter to call your mom; you're not going home tonight." Apart from the fact that the second one would have to be changed because nobody uses payphones anymore, nor do most women live with their parents. Other than that, corny pick-up lines are lovely. What better approach from a man than to churn out some sexist drivel especially for you . . . and your friend . . . and your friend's friend, and so on. Does anyone actually fall for these lines? They used to, like in the 1980s when busy being dazzled by highlighted hair and shiny electric blue suits, but these days such lines can only be a joke. In which case, it's not so bad. But how do you know if he's kidding or not? Easy. Purr back at him, "I like my eggs scrambled," and see what he says. Chances are he'll say, "Uh, I was joking, you weirdo, do you want another drink?" if he's a real man; if not he'll back away slowly and head for the door whilst emitting little squeaks of fear.

Poetry

Now you really don't want this. Trust me. Is he a wolf in sheep's clothing, or just a fool in normal clothing? Poems before he's even bought you a pizza? There's something wrong there. It's bad enough when men write things like "Roses are red, take me to bed," and it's taken them two hours to think it up; actually saying it out loud is unforgivable. It's not 1780. He probably saw it in a film when he was about 13 and decided that was the way forward. Perhaps his mother told him that his dad once read her a poem and that's how he was conceived. It doesn't really bear thinking about. What kind of man does it? A desperate kind who wants to appeal to your romantic side without even knowing if you have one, and who hasn't got the sense to just ask you your name and whether you'd like a drink or not. A decent response to anyone reciting poetry to you in a nightclub would be: "I'd rather drink my own pee than go on a date with thee. You loser."

Speaking in a foreign language

OK, so he could actually be foreign, in which case, don't be too harsh. However, if he's not, and chances are he's only come over to talk to you because he can, uh, *talk*, then he's trying it on. Whispering something in French or Italian is not good. You'll simply hear "Blah blah blah, so, so, so" and have no idea what he's on about. He'll have sworn to his friends, who will all be standing in a group about eight feet away, that it'll work. It's best to view this kind of predator with the utmost contempt. Talk back in Japanese, even if you're only making it up. Better still, if you are Japanese, don't make it up, just tell him to shove off. Ask him what he's saying first, though, just for fun. He'll no doubt reply, "I was saying that I think you're beautiful and fragrant, like a meadow on a summer's day," when in fact he probably said, "A train ticket to Lille and a bathroom with a shower please." Idiot.

The soft-but-predictable approach

Harmless questions such as "Do you come here often?" or "What's your sign?" suggest a distinct lack of imagination, purpose, and confidence. They call for one-word answers, such as "Yes," "No," or "Aries," and whatever follows that will only make you cringe. He'd do better asking what you're drinking, telling you how much money he earns, and giving you some of it so that you stand there and put up with his nonsense. Only the runt of the litter would come out with such pathetic questions, then skulk back to his friends, if he even has any, reporting of yet another failure to capture the heart of a pretty lady. He won't be able to understand what he's doing wrong, so you could always tell him, but it's much more fun to watch him cry instead. At least he's consistent, though—he'll have failed at everything throughout his entire life, and deservedly so. The weak cub at the back of the pack, he'll end up being eaten alive by another male—probably the next woman's boyfriend.

The trying-too-hard tactic

This male will have practised his smile, or even his leer, in front of the mirror for six weeks prior to walking over to you, so he'll have an image of what he thinks he looks like imprinted in his brain. Only he looks like a lunatic rather than the Lothario he imagines he is. After perfecting his "smile," he'll have read tons of men's magazines, which will have given him hundreds of tips on how to pick up a woman, without mentioning that anyone who needs to read a feature in a magazine to tell them how to talk to women has problems so far advanced that nothing will help him. He'll say the same thing to every woman, each sentence embedded in his head with no room for improvisation. "You've got beautiful hair," he'll croon, "just like the colour of the sun," even if your hair is the colour of coal.

The "haven't we met before?" line

No, no, and thrice no. "No" as in "we haven't" but also "no" as in "no, don't say this." What makes a man think this is a clever thing to say? Your response could be any one of the following: a) Yes, at the VD clinic; b) Yes, you're my best friend's fiancé; or, c) No. Whichever answer you give is likely to leave him stumped. In the unlikely event that a woman is daft enough to engage in conversation with a fool

Fig. 6.1 Him: "Do you come here often?" You: "Not anymore."

such as this, she may say, "I don't think so, are you sure?" which then leads him down a long and boring path about where he might have met you, despite the fact that he knows he hasn't met you before and is just struggling to get out of the loop and say, "Can I get you a drink/new handbag/taxi home?" It's probably the most idiotic pick-up line out there. Avoid like the tentacles of a jellyfish.

The silent approach
Not a pick-up line as such, more a way of thinking. The wrong way, that is. He'll just stare at you from across the room. I'm not talking about that fancy thing where men send you a drink and have the barman point to them—this one just stares. He'll expect you to do all the work. If he's like that now, how lazy will he be in a relationship? Very!

HIS PHYSICAL APPROACH

The approach to mating is as important as the act itself. It generally gives us an idea of how the male will perform. A lunge means he'll be clumsy; a gentle touch bodes well for the rest of the night. Here's how to work out what he's thinking by . . .

Leaning in towards you

It's a bit like a shark circling a seal, this one. He's not sure if you're going to punch him in the face or kiss him back. If he has a glass of wine for you in his hand, chances are you're not going to punch him. You're on the sofa, he just went to get you another drink, and when he sits back down, he sits much closer than he was before he got up, with his knees towards yours and his arm on the back of the sofa. You're either going to feel suffocated or excited by this, but at least you're in control. You know whether or not you're going to rebuff his advances–he doesn't. It's a classic non-threatening, gentle approach. If he's impatient and watched too many corny films, he'll take your glass from you and put it on the table, hold the same hand in his, lean in a bit more, and then say something rubbish like, "Shut up and kiss me," to which you'll either do as he says or laugh out loud. It's a move which you can pre-empt, so that's cool. If you don't want to kiss him, you can either cough in his face or tell him you think you're going to be sick. That generally works.

Stroking your face

Are you a cat? Thought not. So what's he doing that for? It's a bit personal if you don't know someone very well, and some women really don't like it, so it's a risky approach. Perhaps he's had a lot of experience with face stroking and rates himself at it. If he's a construction worker or plasterer and has calloused fingers, he really shouldn't try this. He'll say something like, "You know you have beautiful skin/eyes/ears," and you will say, "Oh, these old things," and go all bashful. Then again, he might catch you off guard if he moves too quickly—you could be about to lean in to him and then he'll poke your eye out or get his thumb caught on your earring. Ouch. It's sort of gentle-manly, because it's a very soft approach, but how do you know he's not about to put his hands around your throat and try to strangle you? He's obviously a risk taker, which may lead you to believe that this also makes him untrust-worthy. That could just be paranoia, but if it feels too prac-tised, it probably is.

Putting his hand on your leg

(Fig. 6.2) Like a bear holding down a flapping salmon, his firm hand suggests that he's got you right where he wants you and that he's not likely to let you get away. It's a bit like

Fig. 6.2 Ah, the classic hand-on-knee approach.
Watch out—this fella means business.

the kind of thing old men do to you at work under the table in a business meeting. Well, sort of. It might feel nice, especially if his hand is warm and you've got cold knees, but there's every chance he'll get the wrong idea and put it further and further up your leg until there is nowhere else to go but back down. You can hinder his advances by gently placing your hand on his, then pressing down really, really hard when he gets past the knee. Bend a finger back if he doesn't get the hint after that. It's quite territorial, the placing of the hand, so it suggests confidence, that he's experienced, and that it's probably worked quite well before. A green light from you on this approach and it's full steam ahead.

Fig. 6.3 Is he about to propose or has he dislocated his knee? Either will be painful.

Kneeling in front of you

(Fig. 6.3) Mmm, very subservient. Is he used to begging? Is this how he gets a date in the first place? Perhaps. It might just be that he worships every inch of you and wants to look up to you, literally, and tell you this. He can't kiss you from here, at least not without straining his neck, but he will get a good view if there's any cleavage on show when you lean down, the cunning fox! However, if he's had a lot to drink, he might just put his head in your lap and fall asleep, or worse, throw up. It's a strange and awkward approach, one designed to make you feel special and him feel at your mercy. In reality, it just means he looks really short and gets a cramp, and that's never a good thing. Maybe he is actually really short and isn't kneeling at all. Check to see if his shoes are where you think his knees are. Oh dear.

Approaching from behind

Ugh, what a smooth operator. There's no middle ground here—either you'll like him sidling up to you and nibbling on the back of your neck, or else you won't. Simple as that. He's using an overtly sexual approach, so his confidence is sky high, and he must be reading the signs from you that you're feeling the same. If you're not, you can elbow him in the face quite nicely from this angle. It's a bit of a 1940s film approach, which is sort of nice and old fashioned, but also a bit creepy if you're not expecting it. Check whether he replaced his shoes with slippers for a silent advance. If he did, it's fair to say he's blown it.

Lunging at you

Like a cheetah about to give chase to a gazelle, this is what every woman wants. Honestly. Some men obviously think so or we wouldn't know that they do it. Their theory is probably that they've spent two hours wondering whether to stroke your face, creep up behind you, or tell you to shut up and kiss them. Maybe he's just run out of patience. It's more likely, however, that he's just a pig who's idea of foreplay is to let you in the door and push you on the bed. An absolute no-no, unless, of course, you've been waiting for this moment for weeks. Be careful, though, this could be dangerous. An unexpected lunge can cause all sorts of painful problems. Elbows can enter eye sockets, knees can meet jaws, foreheads can bang against noses—anything can happen. If you're getting up just as he goes for it, you may even clash heads. Only a bold male makes a lunge, and only a woman who stays still escapes without injury.

PREENING
AND PREPARATION

Most species in the animal kingdom spend a lot of time preening before a big date. Birds peck at their feathers, dogs and cats lick their bottoms, and monkeys pick insects from each other's fur. Humans do much the same, but what does his preparation and preening say about him? If he chooses to . . .

Do nothing

(Fig. 6.4) Zero out of ten for effort, hygiene, and general niceness. What's up with him? How can anyone think that doing nothing before a date will get them anywhere? Are you likely to whisper, "Mmm, your neck smells so . . . grimy, like you've been at work all day and then got the subway home," before undoing his tie and ravishing him like there's no tomorrow? Probably not. If he's never put the effort in before, then there's no reason for him to suddenly start, but why should you go to all the bother of washing your hair and painting your nails if he can't even be bothered to brush his teeth? There is, of course, a

Fig. 6.4 Crocodiles stink and have bad teeth, but still go after you. So do some men.

possibility that he's simply not that interested in you. Harsh, but true. He's not exactly out to make you feel special, and the likelihood is that he sees himself as better than you, at least aesthetically, therefore he doesn't need to make the effort–a bit like a crocodile. "How?" you ask. Because they lay in the mud all day sleeping and can only be bothered to move when something they fancy passes right before their eyes. And they stink. And they have bad teeth.

Change his clothes

(Fig. 6.5) Is that it? Is that all you're worth? If he can only find the energy to prepare himself for you this much, it doesn't say a lot about his bed. You know, sheets combined with laundary detergent, that sort of thing. While a change of clothes is better than nothing, it's not *much* better. He's the kind of man who sprays deodorant under his armpits when his clothes are on–you know, a quick burst on both sides, which covers the T-shirt more than the skin, rather than an all-over spray like men in commercials do. If he works somewhere that provides him with a uniform, then he's got to get changed anyway. Even off-duty police officers aren't allowed to roam the streets in their uniforms, so burger joints probably have the same rules. If he changes his clothes it means he likes you a little, but not a lot –unless when he takes you back to his place and says, "I'm sorry, I've got to jump in the shower, I'll be out in a minute," a sure sign that he's after some action. If he comes out of the bathroom in nothing but a towel, he's a bit too keen. If he disappears into the bedroom and puts on clean clothes, he's a gentle-man. Clean and covered up, but fragrant and damp of hair. What more could you ask for?

Fig. 6.5 Men: at least wear a clean shirt.

Have a shower and shave

Fig. 6.6 A shower. It's polite to have one before a date, and it's not exactly asking much, is it?

(Fig. 6.6) This is what you want—the middle ground between underachieving and overachieving, caveman and supermodel. He'll be clean and soft of face, but he won't have put in so much effort that he explodes with rage when you say you're not staying the night. He might have changed the sheets on his bed and put his dirty socks in the laundry basket, but that's what women do all the time, even when they don't have a date. He respects you enough to be clean, is clearly after some kissing at least, and might have something more "intimate" in mind, too, what with him being stubble-free and all. He respects you, wants to smell nice for you, and will probably make you breakfast in the morning—a normal breakfast of eggs and bacon, that is, not heart-shaped pancakes with fresh cream and strawberries, which in the early stages of a relationship is quite scary. You don't want him to use up every trick he knows within the first month, because that's when the "I did all that; I'm not doing it again" thoughts creep into his head.

Buy a new outfit

Is he gay? OK, maybe that's unfair, but maybe it isn't. Panicking about what to wear on a date is a really girly thing to do. The female species sees nothing untoward about spending a few dollars on a new dress and shoes for a second date with someone they like, but a man doing it is just a bit weird—especially the dress part. If he'd just happened to buy a new shirt or jeans, say, that week, without thinking or knowing he had a date, that's OK. But actually going out and consciously spending money on something new is a bit odd. Most men will only go as far as to pick something up from the floor, smell it, make a face, and then wear it anyway. A nice man will put something that smells bad in the wash and find something clean to wear, but not buy something new. It's just not normal. Indecision leading to panic buying means he probably can't read directions or maps and gets really upset when he gets lost, which is rubbish. The woman will end up saying, "I like your shirt," just for something to say, and he'll blow it by replying, "Do you? Do you really? I'm so glad; I bought it especially for our date," which will roughly be translated as "Do you? I'm psychotic!"

Have a facial, manicure, and pedicure

Good grief, are you sure he's not really a woman? That's not right. Really. I know some men see nothing wrong in extensive grooming, but there are many more who believe that it will gradually turn them into a girl, and that their neatly buffed fingernails will next time be painted bright red with little diamonds stuck to the tips. Obvious clues that he's spent time at a spa are really nicely buffed nails and perfect, soft skin that smells like apples or something dodgy like that. A receipt for "Lola's Pampering Parlour" will also give the game away—check the list of items and see if he's had a back, crack, and sack wax while he was at it. It's nice that he cares that much, but it's not that he cares that much about *you*. He cares that much about *him*. Clean fingernails and trimmed toenails are what you want to see, nothing more. There's something a bit suspect about a man who has so much time on his perfect hands that he'd rather spend it in a nail salon than playing pool.

AFTER MATING

The male species knows only two activities really matter in the world: mating and feeding. It's best not to sleep on an empty stomach, which is why men take you out to dinner and then try to have sex with you. But what about after mating? What does it tell us if . . .

He falls asleep

(Fig. 6.7) You'll be cross, but you shouldn't be. It's perfectly natural. God programmed men to sleep when they're happy so that if they die in their sleep, they go peacefully and with a smile on their faces. Or it might be something to do with hormone and serotonin levels after orgasm. Either way, you should count yourself lucky. Who wants to sit up talking all night? He certainly doesn't. You'll only be waiting for him to say, "I love you," and he's probably not going to. He might say thank you before falling asleep, though. That's just weird, as if you're a hooker and you've let him off paying for it. Use this time wisely—don't berate him or huff and puff— either kiss him on the back of the neck or whisper something like "I fancy your friend/dad/brother," to see if he's really asleep, then get up and look

Fig. 6.7 Leave him to it—he can't help it. You can use the time to check out his habitat, or get the hell outta there. . . .

through all his things if you like him or get a taxi if you don't. It's also a good opportunity for you to stare at him for ages to see if you can imagine being his wife. If he drools and snores like a dazed walrus, it's unlikely.

You share a cigarette

This is what happens in cool films, yet nobody ever says, "Ugh, their breath must reek!" or worries about fire-safety regulations. Firemen probably don't smoke in bed; they know better. Watch it if you've got a lot of hairspray going on—you could go up in seconds. Or, indeed, if you're wearing a nightie made from anything other than cotton. There is, of course, the relaxation element to this post-mating activity. Male lions bang away at lady lions for a while, guns blazing, claws firmly in the dust, their mane blowing in the wind. What do they do afterwards? Share a cigarette? Maybe, but my guess is that the male lion lies back in the sun, basking in his glory. A cigarette is a man's way of doing the same, without getting out of bed and lying on the floor. It unites you as one, albeit one who stinks of smoke, and is quite a sexual motion in itself, what with the sucking business. The downside is that you'll probably both die quite soon—either from lung cancer or the bed being set alight.

He gets up to shower

Are you that vile that he has to shower your scent off immediately? Or is he simply repulsed by his own bodily fluids to the extent that he has to bleach himself instead of having a cup of tea and a nice snooze? Some people are put off by the lingering smells, and that's not surprising, but a shower in the morning would usually suffice. Perhaps he has Obsessive Compulsive Disorder. You can tell if he not only cleans himself rigorously but also cleans the bathroom afterwards, moves all the furniture around in the living room, and wipes down all the door handles on his way out. It's better to be clean than dirty, so try not to be offended—instead you should ask to join him. Mind you, if things get heated again in the shower, he'll have to have another one after that as well, and soon he'll wash himself away. His parents were probably really strict and uptight about the mating ritual. You'll have problems with this one.

He asks you what you're thinking

This is a woman's domain, but there are some men who think it's a good idea to say this right after mating. It is not. You'll be thinking one of two things, the first being "I love him," the second being "He's rubbish at doing it," neither of which he'll want to hear. Men think about things like putting up shelves, when his driver's license expires, or how to get you out before his girlfriend comes back. It's a question designed to have no correct answer, and as such is able to ruin a relationship before it's even started. He might be so confident that he's expecting you to say, "I'm thinking that was great sex." Then again, it may go the other way and point to insecurities, which means that anything other than the first reply will lead to him killing himself. Don't say, "I was thinking that you should get a new duvet and not pull that ridiculous face when you climax," unless you want to make him cry.

He tells you he loves you

This is a hard one to work out. Telling you this after mating reaps no reward for him—unlike telling you before, which means you'll probably let him do it. Again, the serotonin levels play a big part in how he acts afterwards, and feelings of lust can be easily misread for those of love. If it's what you want to hear, then great, although if you've just told him that you're about to inherit money or are looking for someone to share a prize of a vacation for two in the Bahamas, it may not be genuine. Making you breakfast or running you a bath is a good indication that he's telling the truth.

BEHAVIOUR
PATTERNS

WITH HIS FRIENDS

How a man acts when he's part of a pack can be very revealing. Is he the quiet one at the back, sipping on his pint and looking at his watch, or the loud one at the bar ordering 107 pints to make himself more popular? So, if . . .

He's the loudest

(Fig. 7.1) Unless all his friends are deaf, there's no need for him to shout. Or is there? Does he feel that unless he makes a lot of noise, nobody will listen to him? If that's the case, it's probably because he doesn't have anything interesting or funny to say, and the only way he can hold their attention is to shout so loud that they have to speak to him, even if it's only to say, "Shut up!" Some men believe what they say is so important that if they don't say it loudly, nobody will take any notice. Watch his hand gestures too—is he always desperate to be the centre of attention, either jabbing

Fig. 7.1 This'll be the loud one of the pack. His friends heard him the first time . . . and the second, and the third. Now he's just being ignored.

his finger at people when he's talking or constantly picking up other people's things? If he really stands out from the group, then it's likely that he's always had problems getting his point across, whether at home or at school or college. He's probably got very little confidence in himself underneath it all, but is unlikely to back down in an argument with you or, more importantly, be able to listen to anything you have to say. All talk and no action.

He's the quiet one

Maybe this is worse than the loud one. What's his role within the group? Does he buy all the drinks? Is he the one who always drives? Maybe he was the one at school who did all the pranks and took the rap, whatever that is? It's usually the quiet ones who spring up in the middle of fights and land the best punches, to everyone's surprise. He might be thinking about what to buy his mom for her birthday, or what to cook for dinner for his girlfriend that night. Then again, he might just be really dull. Watch his friends–do they initiate conversation with him, then wait for a response that never comes? If so, he's not shy–there's something wrong with him. You might think of him as sensitive and broody; someone else may think he's just moody. If he's got a smile on his face, then it's OK–maybe he's just not that interested in what the rest of his friends are talking about. But if he doesn't look comfortable with his own friends, what would he be like with yours?

He always initiates social activity

Is he the kind of male who can't bear to be alone? Does he get bored easily? Has he heard that "only boring people get bored"? It's true. If he finds it impossible to turn down an invitation to something, no matter how bad the activity, then he's afraid to be alone. It means he probably sleeps with a light on and still worries about monsters hiding under the bed. It suggests that he's immature and easily led, and would probably be a pushover in a relationship if he was ever home to have one. It is unlikely that he'd be interested in any form of commitment, as it would interfere with his social life. Constantly ringing his friends and dragging them away from their partners to have a drink or go to a club means that he's probably not very popular with their other halves either. He might have given his heart to a lady once upon a time, had it smashed into pieces, and vowed never to be devoted to a woman again. If you're lucky enough to get time with him but find it hard to pin him down to anything specific, you're wasting your time. He'll only bother calling you when he can't find anyone else to play with.

He prefers one-on-one friendships

(Fig. 7.2) This is more like it. When boys become men they need another male to confide in, to compare tales of their girlfriend's underwear with, and to call up for a beer when they get fired, laid, or dumped. A man with a close friend

Fig. 7.2 What do men in pairs talk about? "Women, eh? My missus ruined my T-shirt—it's covered in bleach."

has someone to hunt with, to travel with, and to swap socks with. It's a fulfilling relationship that bodes well for yours. You may find the best friend hard work at first–he'll be sizing you up, waiting to pick up on anything he doesn't like about you so that he can warn his friend. However, the worst thing that can happen in close friendships vs. relationships is not that the best friend doesn't like you enough; it's that he'll like you too much. You won't want to tell the guy you're dating that his trusty pal has the hots for you, because he's likely to accuse you of flirting with him. He'll stick up for him over you every time. The best friend will also resent you for taking his pal away from him, especially if he's single. Go for a guy with a good friend who has a girlfriend (the friend, that is, not him). That's a healthy balance and one that spells a good future for you. Unless you have to double date all the time and she's a total bore, in which case you're best out of it.

He has no friends

As a child, to have no friends is the worst thing in the world; as an adult, to have no friends is even worse. Children get put in bad clothes by their parents. They get sent to a boarding school in New England because they're too clever to go to their local school in the Midwest, and as a result live nowhere near their classmates. Kids eat worms and weird things like that, which makes it difficult to befriend anyone who doesn't eat worms. An adult with no friends does not have the same excuses– unless he still eats worms, in which case you should give up now. A valid reason for him to be on his own a lot of the time is that all his friends suddenly got married and had kids. If, however, he never mentions anyone who got married and had kids, then it's likely he never had any friends in the first place. Should that be the case, he's going to be more dependent on you than a newborn baby. He'll call you and IM you constantly, he'll get upset when you say you're going out with your friends, and he'll never understand why you "can't just be with him."

WITH HIS FAMILY

How the male behaves around his family will tell you about your potential future with him. If he's nice to his mom, he'll probably be nice to you. If his family disowned him, there might be a good reason. If he disowned them, they might be nudists or something weird like that. So what does it say if . . .

He still lives with them

If he still lives in the same house and he's over 25, you've got problems. Did you really sign up for a relationship with his mom, dad, and little sister? Every time you want a "special cuddle" do you want to have to go to the woods or put a sock in your mouth to keep quiet, praying that his mom doesn't open the bedroom door to see if you want a cup of tea just as you're being slammed up against the headboard? No, didn't think so. No matter how cute he might be, it's never going to work if he hasn't got his own place. It's hard enough meeting a boyfriend's parents for the first time when you've been dating for six months, but meeting them the first time you go out with him is a bit much. If you've got your own place, he'll always want to stay over and leave clothes and a toothbrush there "just in case" (just in case of what? His house burns down?). Within three days he'll have moved in without you even realising it. Tell him to call you when he's grown the nerve to fly the nest, and forget about him in the meantime.

He visits once a week

(Fig. 7.3) That's nice. Like in *The Godfather* when they all go round for supper after killing that guy and burying him in the woods. See, he loved his mom. What better way to round off a murder than by asking your mom to cook you up some spaghetti at midnight? Maybe he's closer to his dad than his mom. If he plays golf with his dad on a Saturday morning, for example, that's really cool. Maybe he drops by on the way back to say hi to his mom, and she gives him some homemade pie to take back and share with you. That's the spirit. You're getting the best of both worlds, then–he's out with his dad rather than his friends, so you won't worry about what he's getting up to, and you get pie as a reward for not quizzing him on where he's been. If, however, he says he's playing golf but you've never seen the golf clubs, you can kill him. If he says they're at his

Fig. 7.3 Golf clubs. If he really plays golf with his dad, he needs a set of these.

dad's, ring his mom and tell her you want to buy him a new set but need to know what brand they are, and she'll say, "I've no idea what you're talking about, dear." A man who is nice to his parents is either about to inherit a fortune or just nice. Either way, you can't go wrong.

He only goes home for Christmas

(Fig. 7.4) What's going on here? Guilt, that's what. He must have done something awful at one point, like date a girl who had her nose pierced or who didn't go to church every Sunday, and although he's never apologised for it because he doesn't believe he was in the wrong, he still feels a bit guilty–hence the once-a-year visit. Obviously, if they just happen to live in another country, it might not be that

Fig. 7.4 Does he only visit his parents' house at Christmas to get a new pair of socks, or is something more sinister afoot?

complicated at all. Or perhaps his parents are the kind who are never satisfied, and even though he's got his own submarine and has a Ph.D. in something you can't even pronounce, they're still disappointed in him. Maybe his older/younger brother/sister is the star offspring, and he feels inferior and unloved. Go with him if you can and find out what the deal is—it might be that they get on fine, but they're just not that close. If that's the case, you haven't really got anything to worry about. It's just like the olden days when people only made one journey a year by donkey because it took them six months to get there and six months to get back.

He's not very nice to them

Uh-oh. Are they lovely people who perhaps fuss around him a lot and treat him like he's still 11 years old? He won't like that. "But mom, I don't need to wear thermal pants; it's July." Mom: "You never know. It could snow and then you would die!" Over-protective parenting, where the little boy has done as he's told and then suddenly realised he's old enough to make his own decisions, equals a man who simply won't take advice from anyone ever again. And you know who he's least likely to listen to? That's right: you. Each time you ask him what time he's going to pick you up or if he's remembered his dental appointment he'll just think, "Leave me alone, woman!" and eventually you will.

He tells you he has no family

(Fig. 7.5) What, was he raised by wolves? This is a man with a big secret. Either he reinvented himself as a man but was born a woman and his family have disowned him/her, or he was the sole survivor in a plane crash in a forest and decided to stay there despite there being no television. If his name rings a bell, run it through the computer in the library, or whatever it is they do in films, and see if any newspaper headlines come up. Ones like, "Boy Raised by Wolves in Forest Relocates to Norfolk" or "Boy Kills Entire Family with Poisoned Milk at Breakfast." It could turn out to be really interesting, but it depends on whether or not you like that kind of "interesting." Alternatively, look at it from the point of view that at least you won't have to buy his parents anything for Christmas—unless, of course, he's still in touch with the wolves, but you can worry about what to buy them nearer the time. It's possible there's something a little less sinister going on—perhaps his parents frequent nudist camps, belong to a weird religious cult, or never allowed him to watch TV.

Fig. 7.5 If he was raised by a family of wolves, Sunday lunch with your boyfriend's parents will be an "unconventional" experience.

MIGRATORY HABITS

When birds decide to head south for the winter, it's simply because it's cold in the north. When the male species heads to warmer climes for summer, it's usually because he wants to see women frolic bikinied in the sea. What does it say about a potential partner if he . . .

Goes away with another single male

This smacks of desperation, particularly if he's gone away with his best friend. "We're only going to lay on the beach," he'll say. Yeah, on top of a naked girl from France, but he won't tell you that bit. Men who migrate in pairs are less threatening than a pack of males, granted, but their predatory instincts grow stronger when they're part of a pair. Many females vacation in pairs, with one usually uglier than the other. This is also true of most males, so they are well matched. The ugly male takes the ugly female, the handsome male the pretty female. Everyone knows their limits, and the ugly ones are thankful for any scraps thrown their way by their better-looking companions. Should a handsome male rather than an ugly one approach you, take it as a sign that you are the prettier of your bunch. Also take it for granted that this male will have done the rounds of every nightspot in town before trying it on with you.

Goes on an extreme sports vacation

(Fig. 7.6) He clearly needs a head rush (or whatever it is men get from throwing themselves off cliffs, out of planes, down foaming rivers, etc.), and this may mean that his relationships are as extreme as his hobbies. He's not going to be happy with a woman whose idea of an extreme sport is to run for the bus or counts talking as exercise. He'll want a girlfriend who doesn't care that her hair gets messed up

Fig. 7.6 A passion for extreme sports means that he'll say unintelligible things like, "I got a top buzz from my drop-bung!"

when she's hanging upside down from a bit of elastic, or who doesn't say, "My nails, my nails!" when he tries to coax her into rock climbing. If he surfs, he's even worse, because his conversation will be littered with phrases you won't understand. He'll say stuff like, "I caught a demon rip wave off the break; it was out there!" or something like that. You'll say, "Pardon? What are you talking about?" and he will leave you. You will mourn his year-round tan and casual way of dressing and combing his hair. He will go out with a girl who looks like him but has firm breasts and can understand what he's talking about. His loss, huh? Well, not really, but never mind.

Goes on vacation with a group of friends

Look out, here they come. An entire pack of hungry wolves, hunting high and low for anything that moves. Is it really that bad? Yes. There will be one male who swears he isn't interested in girls, but by the end of the first night he'll have bumped lips with 17 of them but only remember two. There will be one who is getting married, and he'll sleep with everything, whether it is breathing or not, as "a last gasp for freedom." You will have no idea which way your man will go, other than he's male, so he'll no doubt think that because he's on vacation he can do what he likes because you'll never find out. But men are dumb and take photos of women rather than interesting old buildings or sea creatures. Mind you, some of the women may well resemble sea creatures. One of them will have put a note in his jeans pocket with her address and her name signed with a heart next to it, which is a sure sign that he's been unfaithful. That, along with the hickey, photo evidence of the pair of them in bed taken by his mate, and the fact that all his friends go quiet whenever you see them.

Does nothing but sunbathe

(Fig. 7.7) That's just wrong. George Hamilton and Tom Jones look like the kind of men who do nothing but sunbathe, and who apart from 89-year-old ladies fancies those two? Who wants an orange boyfriend? Who wants to lie on a towel next to a man who keeps moving away from you because he's following the sun to "optimise the tan"? Could you really bear to sit next to a man who wears smaller bikini bottoms than you? Or rolls the top of them down so that he "doesn't get any white parts?" Of course not. You want a man who sits down for five minutes, puts on suntan lotion after he's already covered in sand (which acts as a buffer for what little colour he has), and then stands in the sea for a bit whilst waving at you for no particular reason. Men should turn brown whilst playing volleyball or catching swordfish, not from lying on a sheet of tin foil and spraying themselves with cooking oil. It's wrong, wrong, wrong!

Fig. 7.7 Wrong! Men should wear shorts, not Speedos, and play volleyball, not lie down. A hideous mistake.

Goes away on his own

(Fig. 7.8) Weird men do this, although you have to admire them. Sort of. They say things like, "I just need to find myself," as if they're really lost. "You're in the kitchen," you say, but they don't get it. They take books and swimming trunks and notepads, as though they're going to be so inspired by their loneliness that they write a novel over breakfast one morning. They get really good suntans because there's nobody to put lotion on them, so they burn like hell for three days, then all the burnt bits go brown. By the time they've gotten back to the airport, though, it's already peeling off. Men who enjoy going away on their own are confident and sociable, which are attractive traits, but also liable to vacation on their own all of a sudden, say on a Tuesday, and forget to tell you. They'll use the "I need my space" phrase if you call them more than once a month, and although they probably don't indulge in any romantic activities whilst away, you will always think that they have, simply because there are some women out there with books and notepads who do the same thing and they're bound to cross paths one day. You won't be able to understand why he doesn't want to spend time with you; he won't be able to understand why you don't "get" him. Best not to bother. Males who break from the pack live by their own rules and are usually content with only the sea for company.

Fig. 7.8 The lone wolf. He's just about to find himself, this one.

NOCTURAL ACTIVITY

Does he sleep well, or is he as fidgety as a rattlesnake in a bag? Is the television his romantic interest, or would he rather snuggle up to a cheese sandwich? Find out what his nocturnal habits say about him. If he . . .

Goes straight to sleep

"He sleeps like a baby, always has," his mom would say. You would hope that she means soundly and without turning over every five minutes, rather than on his front in a brushed-cotton onesie. The thing is, most babies cry all night and wet themselves, so I wouldn't take this as a good thing. A man who gets into bed and goes to sleep immediately is one of two things: drunk, or without a care in the world. Or even both. In my experience, a male who is relaxed enough to fall asleep within seconds of his head hitting the pillow can't possibly be anxious about the day ahead of him. His position at work is either so high up the ladder that everything is delegated to his colleagues, or he's in such a lowly position that all he has to fret about is whether there is any coffee in the staff room. You'll have to get him to put his arm around you quickly, before he drops off, or else there's no chance of any cuddles for you.

Watches late-night TV in bed

Has he never heard of saving electricity? Does he not know that too many electrical appliances in the bedroom can give him headaches, not to mention the potential hazard of a bunch of electrical cords to trip over in the dark? It's a bad habit, this one. If it's something he does when he's with you, the chances are that even if you're midway through the throws of passion, a commercial could come on for toilet paper and he'll shout, "That's it! I need toilet paper!" or, worse, a commercial for ice cream with a woman licking it suggestively from a spoon, which makes him gasp in excitement and makes you feel like thumping him on the nose. If he falls asleep with the TV on, you'll have to climb over him to find the remote and turn it off. The remote will be under his bottom. You will give up and have to try to sleep to the sounds of a bad film starring Ray Liotta or someone who used to be in *Melrose Place*. Good luck.

Reads before turning out the light

(Fig. 7.9) This is nice. A wise owl with his little reading glasses, his brain coming to life as everyone else's goes to sleep. A quiet, unassuming gentleman who likes a little relaxation before bed that doesn't come in the form of anything untoward—unless, of course, he's reading *Playboy*, but even that's got proper stories in it. But what is he reading? Men generally like to read autobiographies, biographies, or really bad science-fiction novels. They tend to like things that are "real," such as life stories of their favourite actor or musician, or go completely the other way and read absolute trash about a guy going to Mars in a telephone booth with a harem of beautiful women tending to his every need. That should set him up with some nice dreams. If he's reading the latest blockbuster, then maybe he's a bit of a follower and only reads what other people tell him he should be reading. It's an old-fashioned thing, reading before sleeping,

but it's rather endearing. As long as he doesn't get grumpy when you crawl across the bed for some lovin', he's alright. The minute he says, "Do you

Fig. 7.9 Reading in moderation is OK. Would he rather snuggle up to P. D. James than you? That's worrying.

mind? I'm sure it's a lovely negligee you're wearing but I'm just coming up to the bit where the telephone booth shoots off to space, so can you just go to sleep or at least get off me?" you know you've lost out to literature.

Eats snacks in bed

Does he think he's a lion or something, hunting at midnight and conserving his energy for the day? Because he's not. Snacks in bed equals crumbs in bed; crumbs in bed equals crumbs in your hair and stuck to your bottom. Snacks in bed also goes hand in hand with a fat tummy and an unnerving way about him that suggests he was indulged in too many midnight feasts as a child. Bringing you breakfast in bed on a Sunday morning is not the same as eating chips and cake in bed at 11 p.m. He's unlikely to bother getting out of bed once he's finished snacking to brush his teeth, which means if you want to kiss him it'll be a case of "kiss me, kiss my snacks." Mmm, nice. So what else does it tell you? That he'll probably have a heart attack before he's 40. That he'll be awake half the night with heartburn, which means you'll not get a decent night's sleep either. That when he stays at your place, he'll think nothing of helping himself to a plate of cold chicken and a beer and bringing it to bed as some kind of food foreplay. You could always try to encourage him to eat strawberries and whipped cream, which is slightly sexier than chicken drumsticks. If he'd rather nibble on a dead animal's thigh than yours, he's really not worth the effort.

HIBERNATION INSTINCTS

WHAT FILMS AND TELEVISION HE WATCHES

Apparently, watching films about killing people does not a murderer make. But does watching romantic comedies a romantic comedian make? Probably not. What do his viewing preferences say about him? If he watches . . .

Westerns or police dramas

A proper guy, this one. He hankers for the olden days where you could simply turn up to a town on a horse, park it outside the saloon, drink a bottle of whisky, pick a fight during a poker game, smack the saloon girl on the bottom without getting sued for sexual harassment, shoot someone in the shoulder when he looks at you funny, and then get back on the horse and ride straight outta there. And who can blame a man who wants to live like that? It's perfect. As for police dramas, the reality ones are the best. Sure, *The Shield* and *Law & Order* have their moments, but you can't beat the real police chases and narrative such as "This idiot thought he'd break into the house that just happens to belong to the police chief–instead of getting away with the surround sound TV he gets nabbed." These shows are very funny, and also cool, as well as educational. He won't, for example, now try to break into a house until he's sure it's not occupied by anyone with a firebomb. In the real world, he gets a bus to work and daren't even look at the barmaid at lunchtime, but it's a healthy escapism that served the world well in the 1800s, when men were men, and women were, uh, sexual objects. No change there then. However, if his interests are geared towards *America's Most Wanted* and he gets all fidgety when the "wanted" section comes on, it's a different kettle of fish entirely.

Sports

(Fig. 8.1) A healthy appetite for sports involves 50 percent watching and 50 percent playing. When he's not playing, the 50 percent watching should include grown-up sports where men actually have to be good at running, catching, or whacking things with a stick, such as baseball, basketball, and football. Shooting, wrestling, or skateboarding shows he's still 10 years old in the head, but it's marginally better that he lies on the sofa watching it than actually goes out and does it. A penchant for darts, pool, or golf shows that even his *brain* can't cope with anything fast-moving, let alone his limbs, so it's unlikely he'll ever move from the living room other than to get another beer and some more nachos. You should make yourself scarce when he watches sports, as he'll scream his head off if you happen to walk in front of the television, say to put a small fire out or shut the window when a hurricane is imminent. He'll make a lot of noise, a

Fig. 8.1 Fast cars going round some tarmac. He'll demand to watch it, but he'll be asleep by lap four.

bit like a caveman stabbing a dinosaur would, and crunch beer cans in his hand to show how tough he is. This is why women are programmed to go shoe shopping on Saturday afternoons. Make the most of your genes and get on with it.

Documentaries

"Sssh, be quiet, shut up, go and do the ironing," is what you'll hear if you interrupt him in the middle of a documentary. Is it about gorillas hiding in the bushes, waiting for men with sticks to chase them? Is it about new planets that have been discovered but which look the same as every other planet (lumpy and too hot or too cold, a bit like porridge)? Does he have more of an appetite for learning than he does for noticing you've had your hair cut or have run off with his dad? Perhaps he just has a raging thirst for knowledge, which is preferable to someone with a raging thirst for alcohol. It's likely that he'll be able to help you with crossword clues, and he'd make a good dad because he'd already know lots of things to teach his child before he or she even went to school. At the same time, if you so much as say, "Aw, aren't those gorillas/camels/polar bears cute?" he'll bellow "Wrong! They can kill a man! Shows how long you'd survive in the rainforest/desert/North Pole."

Horror movies

He'll say he's not scared, but he is—otherwise he wouldn't watch them. "Yeah, Freddy Krueger, I could sort him out," he'll say, five minutes before watching *Nightmare on Elm Street*. Twenty minutes into the film he'll be holding your hand and rubbing his brow. Half an hour later he'll be jumping at the slightest noise, such as you getting up to go to the kitchen, and shouting, "Put the light on, put the light on; he might be behind the fridge!" as you get up. Misfortune usually befalls girls early on in horror films, but only after their white tank top has ripped just above their left nipple, or they've been dowsed by a sprinkler in a cold, deserted warehouse. Convenient, huh? If all he watches are horror films, maybe he's just building up character profiles of killing machines and one day hopes to chase you down the stairwell of his apartment with a chainsaw in one hand and a glove with knives attached on the other. Steer clear.

Romantic comedies

What's his problem? It's only girls who are meant to watch this rubbish. If he's got anything with Julia Roberts in it (yes, including *Erin Brockovich*, even though it's not a comedy) then something's seriously amiss. Any man who admits to liking *Pretty Woman*, *Bridget Jones*, or anything starring Hugh Grant should be quarantined. It's not so bad if he secretly watches something over your shoulder whilst pretending to read the paper, but if he actually stands in the video shop and chooses a girly film over one with car chases and big guns, he's either out to impress you by expressing his feminine, sensitive side, or he's gay. I'd lean towards the second option, especially if you spy anything with the words "a spectacular musical treat for the ears!" or "another classic from Walt Disney" on the back cover.

Cartoons

The Simpsons, yes. *Tom and Jerry*, at a push because of its old-fashioned humour. But kids' cartoons that are on in the afternoon or a Saturday morning? That's worrying. Is his brain so tiny that he can only comprehend things that he watched as a child? Perhaps he needs the stimulation of lots of different voices and expressions to keep him awake, or even alive. Does he have no desire to learn anything other than how the Incredible Hulk looks really bad when someone draws him but really good when he's a real guy on TV? *Teenage Mutant Ninja Turtles* is forgivable, just for the title, but anything else is really disturbing. When the cartoons stop, he probably gets out his crayons and colouring books. Liable to say "zowee!" or "bam!" when he thinks you look pretty or he's just killed a spider. Unlikely to understand the plot of *Titanic*.

WHAT COMPUTER GAMES HE PLAYS

Just because he plays football games on the computer doesn't mean he's sporty, but if he plays war games it may mean he's harbouring a secret desire to join the Marines. What else does what he plays say about him? If he plays . . .

Fig. 8.2 Aside from the microwave, this is man's most treasured tool. He may not know how to press your buttons, but he'll be more than competent with these.

Sports games

A love of football via the Xbox or PlayStation does not automatically make him a sports genius. You will realise this as soon as he lies down on the sofa at 6 p.m. and doesn't even so much as sit up until 1 a.m. We all know that the male species can only concentrate on one thing at a time, so while they're immersed in scoring touchdowns for the Dallas Cowboys or throwing themselves around a digitally reproduced muddy field with a pointy ball tucked under their armpit, don't expect a conversation. Video games show they've an interest in sport but are essentially too lazy to get up and leave the house to take part in the real thing. The only exercise they get is in their thumbs, which isn't quite the same as a 90-minute basketball game. It's also likely that because it's a sports game they'll find it necessary to drink 12 cans of beer and eat five bags of chips, as if they're watching a real game. He'll also probably call you into the room every five minutes to show you "his touch-down." You will be able to feign interest for approximately three seconds before screaming, "It's not a real touchdown, you idiot!" and leaving him for someone who actually plays the real thing. If there is such a thing as computer chess, you don't need me to tell you what that says about him.

Combat/war games

Is he 14 years old? There's something about the whole shooting and shouting thing that most women find quite disturbing, and with good reason. It either means he's got a violent streak that he can't be bothered to satisfy by going to the gym and punching the hell out of one of those ball things on a chain, or he'll say he always wanted to join the army but "had a knee injury." War games make a lot of noise as well, not just on screen but also via him. Hearing random phrases shouted at the computer while you make a cup of tea may cause an accident and is not the kind of small talk you'll have had in mind when you popped round to see him. There's something pretty juvenile about a grown man pretending to shoot or blow up computer-generated men for fun, but it's marginally better than doing it for real. It is likely, however, that a couple of hours of this will make him aggressive and unable to sleep. It will quite possibly give him bad dreams during which he grabs your throat and says, "Don't come any closer or I'll blow your head off!" which isn't exactly romantic.

Platform games

These are weird. They show an aptitude for being able to press buttons that make you bend your legs and spring upwards, but they're not exactly the most macho games out there. It shows that in real life he might be quite useful if he is being chased up fire escapes or across roofs of tall build-ings, but it's unlikely that his thumbs will be able to control him in that situation. It's just a bit lame, hopping from one thing to another, and shows a lack of adventure, which could mean that he's a bit dull in the sack. If he's got bunk beds, he'll be great at climbing up to the top one or jump-ing from one bed to another in a hotel room, but that's about it. As exciting as tidying up your sock drawer.

Beat-'em-up games

This is more like it—the hands-on approach of a real man. Well, a man who plays computer games; but better that than him going off in the middle of the night to beat up people for real. There's the martial arts side of it, which shows imagination, flair, and grace, and there's the sucker punches to the bad guy's head, which frankly just shows brute force and a love of confrontation. He'll know what to do if you're about to get mugged, but if he does land a punch it may sur-prise him when the mugger's head doesn't fly off. He'll also wonder why he doesn't get 50 bonus points for smacking that guy in the mouth. You know, the one who looked at you for 0.7 seconds and almost smiled in your direction. Instead of points and flashing gold stars he'll get a $250 fine and 30 hours community service.

Old-school arcade games

(Fig. 8.3) A love of retro games such as Pac Man shows a sentimental side to this male. He hankers for the days when he could pop to the arcade on a Saturday morning and spend his pocket money on a couple rounds of Space Invaders and some penny candy. Sadly, those days are gone, unless he's quit his job because of his addiction to arcade games, which wouldn't be good. Does he ride around on a Chopper bike and wear the same sneakers he had when he was 10 years old? If so, he might be making too much of an effort to be trendy, or at worst, be so fixated on being 10 years old again

Fig. 8.3 Old-school arcade games require the male to stand up, thereby exercising both his legs and his hands.

that he also wets his pants when he laughs too much, eats nothing but chocolate, and fantasises over the girl next door. Eek. If he enjoys winning fluffy orange ducks for you at the local fair and taking you on the bumper cars, then it's harmless. If he actually wants to work there, then you're in trouble. Come to think of it, if he does work at the arcade, it could hinder your career progression, as he'll have one of those special keys that unlock the coin slot and you'll get to play Space Invaders all day for free. Cool, huh?

WHAT MUSIC
HE LISTENS TO

Does he walk around the house looking like Eminem despite the fact that he's been to boarding school and has a Ph.D.? Does he listen to nothing but heavy metal, which means he can only converse by growling really loudly and nodding his head up and down in a vigorous manner? According to Nietzsche, life without music is an error, so what does the kind of music a guy is into say about him? If he listens to . . .

Hip-hop

(Fig. 8.4) Does he call you his "bitch"? I would hope not, but even if he doesn't say it out loud, he probably says it in his head, or to his friends, or on a tattoo across his chest. Does he flick his fingers like a rap star when things go well and suck his teeth when they don't? Proper rap stars drink lots of Cristal Champagne and wear too much gold. And diamonds. And baggy tank tops underneath ill-fitting overalls. He might be a quiet, sensible hip-hop lover who just likes the music and doesn't feel the need to act or dress the part; in which case, that's fine. He'll probably have a little dance in a club now and again, but he is unlikely to spend the entire night checking his reflection in mirrored walls and blinding himself with the glare of diamonds against glass. Affected hip-hop mannerisms are hideous—if he really is in a gang in LA, then fair enough if he wants to wear a bandanna in his back pocket and jeans nine sizes too big. However, if he works in IT, lives at home with his parents, and still talks to you like he's 50 Cent, then you'll have no choice but to laugh and walk away. He'll think he's a big strong lion with an attitude to match; you'll think he's about as tough as a gerbil.

Indie

Is his CD collection full of bands you've never heard of? Does he pride himself on only liking records that haven't made the charts? Maybe he scoffs at your lack of knowledge of the "real" indie scene when you say you used to like Oasis and think Coldplay is cool. He'll say, "If it's on the radio or TV, it's not cool anymore," despite the fact that he's in a band that practises in his mate's garage and would kill for the chance for one of their dreadful songs to be on hospital radio, never mind MTV. He might be alright and just like listening to proper music with guitars and flutes and stuff instead of noises made by drum machines, and it's quite nice to have a man who can sing things at you instead of doing that human beat-box thing in his bedroom. If he picks that up, hide.

Sure, he might have a nice voice, but it's unlikely, and the embarrassment of having him sing to you quite badly outweighs the risk that you might miss something good.

Folk

What's wrong with him? Listening to folk music, that's what's wrong with him. What does he mean when he says he likes it? What's to like? A bunch of hippies mindlessly plucking away at a harp and banging tambourines with someone in the background making a noise like a cat when you tread on its foot? He will wear beads. Recycled beads, that is. And probably believes that you shouldn't shave your legs

Fig. 8.4 A folk musician's favourite: the lute. If he has one of these, hit him with it, and then run away. Quickly.

WHERE HE HIBERNATES

"I need my space," he'll whine, but where will he choose to relax and unwind away from the clutches of female predators?

In his bedroom

The classic hiding place. If bears could put duvet covers on, they wouldn't spend six months of the winter sleeping in the woods wrapped in bits of fern and old newspaper. Come to think of it, how many members of the male species can put duvet covers on? Not many. That's why most males don't bother changing their bed sheets. It's not that they can't be bothered to wash them; they don't know how to put it all back together. So does he retreat to bed for hours on end, ignoring your calls or your mugs of hot chocolate, which are left to go cold outside the door? Maybe he's just not warm enough and doesn't have enough sweaters so he wears his duvet instead. He's trying to tell you something here, though–and that something goes along the lines of "Leave me alone, I want to sleep, then sleep a bit more, then after that I might sleep for a bit." Do as he says, and pray that he will rise again and have a shower shortly after. The laziest of all hibernating males, this one. Also a sure sign that he'd climb straight back into his mother's womb if he was small enough.

In his living room

(Fig. 8.6) This isn't so bad. At least he's out of bed. He's probably eating, although it'll be takeout food so there is bound to be a mound of tin-foil dishes with remains of pork lo mein, not to mention a scattering of cardboard boxes housing mouldy slices of pizza. Although it may appear fairly harmless at first glance, living-room hibernation is quite dangerous. It means he's not sleeping–quite probably

Fig. 8.6 Yes, he can hear the phone. Yes, he knows it's you.
No, he's not going to answer it.

the opposite. At least Bed Hibernation Man will be getting some rest and recharging his batteries; Living Room Hibernation Man will just be watching really bad daytime television, quite bad early evening television, and then even-worse-than-daytime late-night television. He will have square eyes and a round tummy. Does the phone ring for ages, before going on to the answering machine? Have you left more than 12 messages in one day? He can hear you, you know, when you say, "Dave, pick up, it's me. I know you're there." See, he knows you're there as well, but he doesn't want to talk to you. A week of this behaviour should be enough to put you off—any longer and by the time he snaps out of it you'll find yourself dating an agoraphobic, obese, pasty-faced male with old food stuck to his socks.

Fig. 8.7 An empty bar stool beside a full one? This is a man
who needs his space and his drink.

At the bar

(Fig. 8.7) He doesn't want to be alone, but he doesn't want
to be with you, either. This is almost worse than him hibernating and shutting down completely. OK, so it's less
mental, but it means he's fully functioning on the social side
of things and just doesn't want to socialise with you. Oh
dear. If you know which bar is his regular haunt, it may be
that you could spy on him. Is he in a corner by himself nurs-
ing a bottle of bourbon with a book called *How to End Your
Life Without Making Too Much Mess*? If so, go and buy some
new shoes or something nice instead of interrupting him. If
he's with a group of friends, he really, really isn't interested
in you at all anymore. Don't approach the pack at any cost—
you'll be like a lamb to the slaughter. He'll have told his
friends that he's trying to hide from you, that he's not
returned any of your calls, and that he thinks your hair is too
big/breasts too small/dress sense like that of a clown. His
friends will snigger and you will cry. Messy.

At his mom's

It's no fun being a dad, what with having to put up shelves and drive teenagers to parties, but it's even worse being a mom. They're the ones who have to console their offspring when they're upset, or in this case, hiding from you. She'll tell him to face up to it and call you. He'll say he doesn't want to. She will think him weak as a kitten. She will be right. She will feel sorry for you, even though she has never met you. "That poor girl," she'll say, "just ring her and put her out of her misery." He'll pretend to take her advice, but inside he knows he will just keep stringing you along until you get bored or leave the country. This is the weakest type of hibernating male, retreating to the bosom of his mommy for comfort. She'll forgive him for being such a wimp, which means he'll think he can always get away with treating a woman badly as long as his mom still loves him—a bit like a toddler who has a tantrum, holds his breath, almost dies, screams "I hate you!" and still gets a cuddle. Pathetic.

You have no idea where

Uh-oh, this spells trouble. If he tells you he needs to get away for a while, but doesn't tell you where, then your budding relationship is in serious bother. Unless he works for the CIA and isn't allowed to tell you where he's going for fear of having to kill you, then there's no excuse. Does he think you'll keep bothering him while he's clearing his head? He's probably right. Women do that a lot. Maybe it's a lot simpler than that, though, and all you have to fret about is that he does, in fact, have a wife and several children. Or a child and several wives. Either way, it doesn't look good. Should he return with a tan, that's a different story. He's just too mean to pay for you to go on vacation with him. Or he owns a tanning salon, which you don't know about for tax reasons. Don't puzzle over it for too long; simply get the hint and look for another mate.

GLOSSARY OF TERMS

256 The total number of bits of paper he'll have written your telephone number on if he likes you in case he loses it.

Alco-pops Coloured water with a bit of vodka in it? Why would a grown man choose to drink such a thing? Slamming down a pint glass in anger is one thing–throwing an empty bottle of watermelon-flavoured water across the room is another.

Bandanna Worn by the "crims" in Michael Jackson's "Beat It" video to make them look scary. It did, but for the wrong reasons.

Cartoon-character socks Cotton at its most evil. The wearer thinks of himself as "crazy" and "out there." Avoid at all costs, unless you want to see his Homer Simpson boxers.

Celtic symbols On ancient buildings, not so bad; on the arms of idiotic men, very bad. They mean nothing, yet adorn many arms and bases of spines the world over. Tattoo artists should use poisoned ink when someone requests one of these.

Circular dance The celebratory ritual dance of males when they score goals or successfully pick up a lady.

Colour-coded clothes hanging Wrong, wrong, wrong. What is his wardrobe used for? An Ikea storage-solving photo? If he could hang his clothes in alphabetical order, he'd do it. Tidy is one thing; insane is another.

Crazy As in a man who thinks he's crazy in a "funny" way, rather than crazy in a lunatic asylum way. He is not. See also "Cartoon-character socks."

Fungal infections Usually of the feet, but sometimes of the nether regions. You'll have an idea of any fungal history from a glance in the bathroom cabinet.

Gadgetry The latest toy in his collection–moving on from *Star Wars* figures (maybe) and Smurfs, he's now progressed to a phone that lets him programme the microwave for his dinner.

Hawking sound The panic-stricken squawk emitted from the mouth of a man who doesn't want you to touch his new camera phone in case you leave dirty fingerprints on it or move it outside the only square inch within seven miles where it can pick up a signal.

Kiss my snacks A man who eats late at night but is too lazy to clean his teeth afterwards, so you are forced to kiss his snacks, not just him.

Novelty toilet seats So desperate to impress you that he buys a new toilet seat that is more exciting than his personality.

Out there See also "Crazy."

Pompadour Another name for a quiff, as in Elvis's hairstyle in the 1950s. Pure sex, pure male, pure mess on the pillows.

Romantic comedies The choice of millions of women worldwide when deliberating over what DVD to rent in Blockbuster. Should under no circumstances be the male's choice. He should choose films about martial arts or zombies.

Rope-like We're talking dreadlocks, and when I say rope, I mean rope that has been left outside an unused garage for six months and seen rain, snow, and intense sunlight, not to mention mice, fleas, and crumbs dropped from the beaks of passing birds.

Shark's tooth necklace "Look, I was swimming in Bermuda and all of a sudden a great white attacked me! I punched it in the face and killed it, dragged its corpse ashore, and kicked out its teeth. I gave some of the teeth to the local kids and kept the big one for myself." Oh, really? "No. I bought it at Target." Exactly.

Van Gogh's Sunflowers A bad painting. I don't mean technically (although I've always thought it was rubbish), but who wants a man whose imagination stretches to a copy of a famous painting rather than something that inspires his imagination or his own paintbrushes?

Vertically challenged Short. Not tall. A man of less than average height who generally has spiky hair to make himself appear taller.

Wallet An empty one is bad news. One with lots of credit cards in it is also bad news. It doesn't mean he's rich; it just means he needs lots of credit cards. Credit cards in someone else's name is even worse.

QUICK-REFERENCE GUIDE

Sometimes us ladies need an emergency trouble-shooting guide to what's hot and what's not—and I don't mean in the world of fashion. OK, so this book serves as a best friend, issues warnings and advice, and should keep you from making terrible mistakes such as dating a man who owns cowboy boots or keeps corpses under his bathroom floor. But what about when you only have a split-second to make up your mind about a man? That's when this section comes into its own. Here are some definite dos and don'ts:

Making the first move

Do: Avoid approaching a man who looks like he's with his girlfriend. If you're not sure, smile at him. If he smiles back, he may be with his sister. If you get a punch in the face, it was his girlfriend. Assume girlfriend for safety's sake. If he's interested, he'll come over to you.

Don't: Approach a male in a pack. He may be in the midst of taking bets on whether he should ask out you (the pretty one) or your friend (the not-so-pretty one). Or vice versa. You might think you're the pretty one; they might not. It will only end in tears.

Do: Look at his feet. If he's wearing cowboy boots, run for your life. He's in midlife crisis stage two (stage one is the sports car but he's probably had to sell that to pay for the cowboy boots).

Don't: Go for a man with hair longer than yours. If he's got black hair, he wishes he was Marilyn Manson; if it's blonde, he wishes he was Marilyn Monroe. Neither is a good option.

If he invites you to his place

Do: Take note of the smell as you enter the kitchen or bathroom. Anything remotely resembling death, or at least rotting carcasses, is bad news. If the trash bag moves and squeaks, call a taxi.

Don't: Say you'll spend the night before you've had a chance to inspect his bedroom. An unmade bed is one thing; a bed covered in dog hair, another lady's hair, blood, sweat, or tears is not conducive to a good night's sleep, nor anything else for that matter.

Do: Check his closet, if he has one. If he's got a portable thing with stupid linen curtains across the front or just a crappy old rail with shirts on it, then he's either on the run or commitment-shy. If he can't commit to a proper closet, will he be able to commit to you? Unlikely.

Don't: Open the fridge unless you're prepared to be horrified. Chances are that, instead of being full of Champagne, olives, and fancy cheeses, it'll be full of sour milk, half-drunk cans of supermarket-brand beer, and some unidentifiable green fluff which may have once been a tomato.

After mating

Do: Let him go to sleep. It's natural. Something to do with hormone levels. Use this time to call a taxi if you've gone off him, or rifle through his belongings if you intend to make a habit of it.

Don't: Ask him what he's thinking. He'll be thinking that he could do with renewing his car tags or getting some quality time in on his Xbox the minute you fall asleep.

Do: Share a cigarette–but only if you smoke. It looks cool in films but in reality makes your breath smell terrible. However, it's a nice end to what was hopefully a nice few minutes/hours of passion.

Don't: Fall asleep without putting the cigarette out. You don't want to set the bed alight, even if you are fortunate enough to have bagged yourself a fireman. After all, he is off duty.

INDEX

A

alcoholic 39, 62–3, 64

B

bars 34, 62
bathrooms 54–6
bed 46–7, 82, 134, 141
bedroom 46–9
body language 28, 30–3, 35
books 44–5, 47
  reading 47, 119–20
  recipe 53
  self-help 44–5

C

cars 6, 16, 39, 79, 84
chauffeur 39, 81
Christmas 111–12
coffee 50, 61, 76, 83
computer games 126–9
condoms 47
construction worker 77–8

D

drinks 62–5
  alco-pops 64, 138
  beer 62
  cocktails 33, 52, 65
  spirits 63–4
  vodka 24, 52, 62–3

E

ex-girlfriends 22, 53, 54, 55–6, 71
eye contact 35, 37

F

firemen 75, 82, 103, 141
first approach 94–7, 140
flowers 40, 78
food 58–61, 141
  breakfast 66–7, 68, 100
  cooking 51–2, 58, 68
  eating 66–9
  eating in bed 120
  fast food 27, 60–1
  lunch 67–68

  obtaining 70–2
  takeout 50, 59–60, 134
  vegan 61
football 21, 28–9, 35

G

gentleman 20, 27, 95
glasses 47
golf 111
hairstyles 7, 12, 14–17, 32, 35
  blonde 15
  dreadlocks 14, 15
  greasy 133
  highlights 16, 81, 90
  long 15

H

handcuffs 37
hibernation 134–7
hunting (in packs) 15, 35, 36–7, 115–16

J

jeans 11, 12, 13,
  21, 61,
  baggy 131
  tight 133
jewellery 24

K

kitchens 50–3
kissing 28, 35, 36,
  37, 64, 70, 94,
  96, 97, 100, 102,
  120, 139

L

linen 11
lies 44–5, 63, 74

M

magazines 44–4, 46,
  54, 81, 92
mama's boy 19
marriage 28–9, 85,
  115
midlife crisis 88
mother 7, 16, 29,
  36, 58, 70, 107,
  110–11, 112, 137
motorbike 40, 133
music 23, 130–3
  collection 44

N

novelty socks 8, 10,
  138

P

packs (hunting in)
  15, 35, 36–7,
  115–16
parents 10, 37, 70,
  87–8, 104, 109,
  110–13, 137
personal assistants
  82–3, 84
phones 18, 22, 26,
  29, 67, 77, 135
pick-up lines 90–3
plumage 9
poetry 90–1
policemen 76, 82
porn 44, 58, 67
preening 32,
  98–101
pyjamas 10

R

reading 47
real estate agents 74
restaurants 27, 71
retro 43, 53, 129

S

serial killer 7, 47,
  68
shoes 12, 15, 18–21,
  61
short men 15, 97
skateboards 13, 38
sleep 102–3, 118,
  141
smile 35, 37, 92

smoking 103, 132,
  133, 141
sneakers 18
sports 123–4, 127
students 80, 86–7
suits 12, 77, 90
suntan 21, 115, 116,
  117
sweaters 8, 11

T

takeout 50, 59–60,
  134
tattoos 12, 76, 138
television 60, 87,
  113, 118–19,
  122–5, 135
transport 38–40

U

unemployment
  86–8
uniforms 74, 75, 99

V

vacations 78, 114–17
vodka 24, 52, 62–3

W

wages 78–81, 91
wallet 7, 23, 31, 81,
  139
work 13, 67–8,
  74–7, 118, 122,
  131
  ambitions 82–5

ABOUT THE AUTHOR

Juliette Wills is a 30-something-year-old freelance journalist from Brighton, England, who has, by her own admission, "had the misfortune to have dated a wide range of specimens from the male species—rich, poor, fat, thin, tall, short, ugly, handsome, losers, winners—every type imaginable in my quest to find someone who's not insane or more in love with himself than he is with me."

Juliette's insider knowledge of the male species comes from 10 years of working on magazines like *Loaded*, *Marie Claire*, and *Q*. During this time she has written about sports, film, and music, and—as a columnist for the *Guardian* newspaper—soccer.

Her ideal man would be a cross between Johnny Depp circa 1986 and Elvis Presley circa 1956 and be able to cook a roast dinner, fix her car, and pay for her shoes.